Copyright 2016

Contents

-
-
-

Introduction   5

-

Lawsuits   11

-

Poems   97

-
-

Introduction

    I hate long introductions, so I'll make this one short. I had chanced upon Riches one night in the first and last place one would think to find such fringe greatness – deep in the bowels of YouTube. It was a video he had recorded of himself pulling into a McDonalds drive-thru and attempting to order "weapons" and "mustard gas." He had a printout of James Holmes' face taped to his steering wheel. I watched all of his videos hungrily that night, and I wondered, from whose deranged mind had all this hatched? Who was this man? – and *what did he know*? The voice from behind the camera introduced itself as being that of Jonathan Lee Riches. The name stuck immediately.
    By this time, Riches had already a small but loyal fan base. He had only just been released from prison, I had learned, having served a ten-year sentence as a result of credit card fraud, surfing the then rising tide of "phishing" crime. While in prison, it would seem that he began forging lawsuits towards the middle of his sentence to find some way to entertain himself while on the inside – and maybe entertain those on the outside, too. As legend would have it, in May of 2009, Riches sued the Guinness Book of World Records when he heard that they were listing him as "the most litigious individual in history."
    If art's highest purpose is, as some would say, "to disturb the comfortable and comfort the disturbed," then Riches' work is nothing less than that of a Great Artist. The lawsuits, Riches says, are sent out in an effort to "flood the system," to throw a monkey wrench into the clockwork of bureaucracy. They are far more than mere entertainment, although, in a culture that is so largely defined by its avenues of entertainment, they can also work on that level alone. And although some of the more bizarre, outrageous suits are reproduced here in this book,

they are only a small fraction of the two-and-a-half thousand (and counting) Riches has filed since his first in January of 2006.

If the purpose of this book is to compile and celebrate Riches' body of work, to share it and help to keep it in remembrance, then it will hopefully go down in History as a proper testament to the balls of the man – for Riches is nothing less than a god among trolls, an artist and poet, indubitably.

Michael Sajdak, Editor

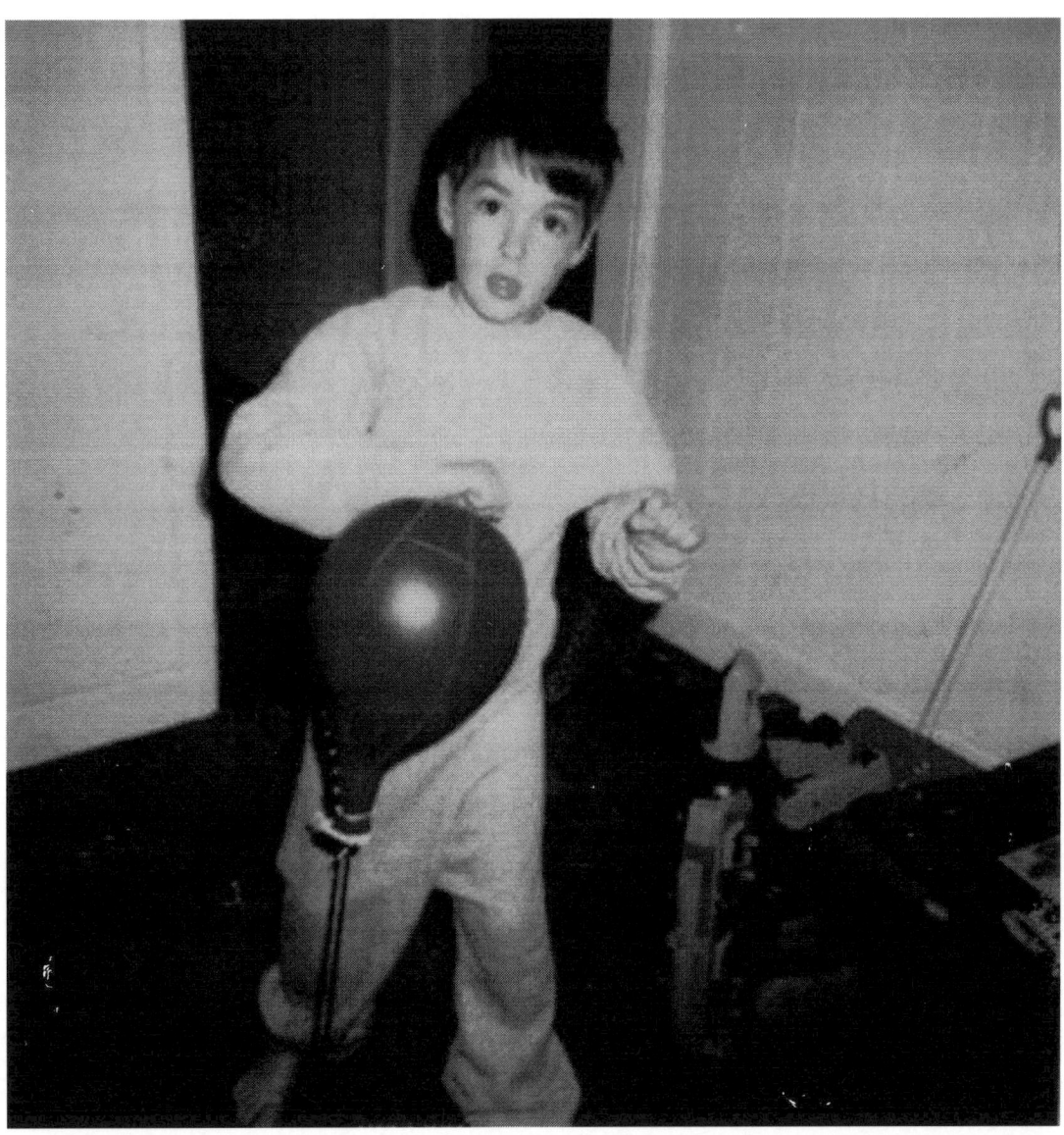

Lawsuits

LP

IN THE UNITED STATES DISTRICT COURT
FOR THE EASTERN DISTRICT OF PENNSYLVANIA

06 -1055

FILED
MAY 9 2006
MICHAEL E. KUNZ, Clerk
By _____ Dep. Clerk

Jonathan Lee., Riches©,
PLAINTIFF,

CASE NO:

VS

GEORGE W. BUSH, individually and in his Official capacity as PRESIDENT of the UNITED STATES OF AMERICA; RICHARD B. CHENEY, VICE PRESIDENT; CONDOLEEZA RICE, SECRETARY of STATE; DONALD H. RUMSFELD, DEPARTMENT of DEFENSE; JOHN W. SNOW, SECRETARY of TREASURY; unknown authors of the UNIFORM COMMERCIAL CODE "UCC"; CARLOS M. GUTIERREZ; SECRETARY of COMMERCE; MICHAEL O. LEAVITT, SECRETARY of HEALTH and HUMAN SERVICES; ELAINE CHAO, SECREATARY DEPT. of LABOR; STEPHEN L. JOHNSON, ADMINISTRATOR ENVIROMENTAL PROTECTION AGENCY (EPA); MARGARET SPELLINGS, SECRETARY DEPT. of EDUCATION; SAMUEL W. BODMAN, SECRETARY of ENERGY; NORMAN Y. MINETA, SECRETARY DEPT. of TRANSPORTATION; HILLARY RODHAM CLINTON, SENATOR of NEW YORK; JAMES HOFFA, PRESIDENT INTERNATIONAL BROTHERHOOD of TEAMSTERS; www.GOOGLE.com; POPE BENEDICT XVl; KINGDOM OF SAUDI ARABIA; JERRY WEST, VICE PRESIDENT of the LOS ANGELES LAKERS; www.ACCUWEATHER.com; USAMA BIN LADEN a/k/a "USAMAH BIN-MUHAMMAD BIN-LADIN"; WILLIAM GATES, CHAIRMAN of MICROSOFT; HUGO CHAVEZ, PRESIDENT of VENEZUELA; JOHN DEERE tractors; ADOLF HITLER'S, NATIONAL SOCIAL-IST PARTY; ISLAND DEF JAM MUSIC GROUP, ROC-A FELLA RECORDS, SHAWN CARTER d/b/a "JAY Z"; QUEEN OF ENGLAND; JO ANNE B. BARNHART, COM-MISSIONER OF SOCIAL SECURITY; STEVEN SPIELBERG; RJ REYNOLDS TOBACCO HOLDINGS INC; JAPAN'S NIKKEI STOCK EXCHANGE; GAMBINO crime family; THREE MILE ISLAND, NUCLEAR POWER PLANT; KOFI ANNAAN, SECRETARY GEN-ERAL UNITED NATIONS; TONY DANZA; ISLAMIC REPUBLIC of IRAN; DON KING PRODUCTIONS INC; PARIS HILTON; KINGDOM HALL of the JEHOVAH'S WIT-NESS; JOSE PADILLA; UNIVERSITY OF MIAMI; GEICO insurance; VIENNA CONVENTION; MATT DRUDGE, "THE DRUDGE REPORT"; MARION BLAKEY, ADMIN-ISTRATOR FEDERAL AVIATION ADMINISTRATION "FAA"; CONSULATE GENERAL of NIGERIA; THE SALVATION ARMY; JEWISH STATE of "ISRAEL"; JOHN E. POTTER, POSTMASTER GENERAL UNITED STATES POSTAL SERVICE "USPS"; SOLEDAD O'-BRIEN, MILES O'BRIEN, co-anchors "AMERICAN MORNING, CABLE NEWS NET-WORK "CNN"; MAGNA CARTA; TSUNAMI victims; ALAN GREENSPAN, former FED-ERAL RESERVE CHAIRMAN; THE AMERICAN RED CROSS; MARK EMERSON, COMM-ISSIONER of INTERNAL REVENUE SERVICE "IRS"; JESSICA ALBA; SIRIUS SATELLITE RADIO; CHARLES MOOSE, former MONTGOMERY COUNTY MARYLAND POLICE CHIEF; DALAI LAMA; THE HOUSTON CHRONICLE; AL QAEDA ISLAMIC ARMY; FRUIT of A-LOOM; AMERICAN CIVIL LIBERTIES UNION "ACLU"; OUT-BACK STEAKHOUSE; DONALD J. TRUMP, TRUMP PLAZA; CHRIS BERMAN of ESPN; THE VATICAN; SHAWN JOHN COMBS d/b/a "PUFF DADDY" d/b/a "DITTY"; MICH-AEL BROWN, former DIRECTOR of FEDERAL EMERGENCY MANAGMENT ADMINISTRA-TION "FEMA"; VINCENT K. MCMAHON, CHIEF EXECUTIVE OFFICER of WORLD WRESTLING FEDERATION "WWF"; THE TALIBAN; RICHARD M. DALEY, MAYOR of CITY of CHICAGO; MEALS on WHEELS; JOHN GRISHAM; COLUMBINE HIGH SCHOOL; ARIEL SHARON, former HEAD of ISREALI LIKUD PARTY; UNITED PARCEL SERVICE "UPS"; TARA REID; BLACK ENTERTAINMENT TELEVISION INC "BET"; SADDAM HUSSEIN; JEWISH workers at NBC/UNIVERSAL; BRAD PITT, and his adopted son MADDOX PITT/JOLIE; JACK WELCH, FORMER CEO of GENERAL ELECTRIC and SUBSIDIARIES; ELIZABETH SMART; GEORGE E. PATAKI, in his Official ca-pacity as GOVERNOR of NEW YORK; CHARLIE SHEEN; THE SURGEON GENERAL

VLADIMIR PUTIN, PRESIDENT of RUSSIA; OLIVER NORTH; GEORGE ORWELL; www.ASKJEEVES.com; SEAN O'KEEFE, former ADMINISTRATOR of NATIONAL AERONAUTICS and SPACE ADMINISTRATION "NASA"; THE KREMLIN; DAVID LETTERMAN; THE PANAMA CANAL COMMISSION; GEORGE J. TENET, former DIRECTOR of CENTRAL INTELLIGENCE AGENCY "CIA"; KELLY CLARKSTON; THIRTEEN TRIBES of ISRAEL; AMERICAN HEART FOUNDATION; PLATO; LINCOLN MEMORIAL; OCCUPATIONAL SAFETY and HEALTH ADMINISTRATION "OSHA"; BORIS BECKER; FREEMASON LODGE; EGLIN AIRFORCE BASE; various BUDDHIST MONKS; www.SECUREDPARTY.com; I. LEWIS "SCOOTER" LIBBY, FORMERCHIEF of STAFF to VP DICK CHENEY; WARREN BUFFETT, CEO BERKSHIRE HATHAWAY; SIERRA CLUB; JOHN D. NEGROPONTE, AMBASSADOR to UNITED NATIONS; CHRISTINA APPLEGATE; JEWISH MOSSAD; NATIONAL VANGUARD BOOKS "NVB"; AIR and SPACE MUSEUM; CHRISTOPHER REEVES widow; GALE A. NORTON, SECRETARY of INTERIOR; HALLIBURTON COMPANY, KELLOGG BROWN & ROOT; JOHN WALSH, HOST of AMERICA'S MOST WANTED; MEIN KAMPF; CITY of CRAWFORD TEXAS; JOHN P. ABIZAID, GENERAL COMMANDER U.S. CENTRAL COMMAND; VENUS WILLIAMS; www.DEFCON.org; JOHN DUDAS, DIRECTOR PATENT and TRADEMARK OFFICE; MEDIEVAL TIMES; INTERNATIONAL TRADE COMMISSION "ITC"; ANNA NICHOLE SMITH; UNITED STATES MARINE CORPS.; WILLIAM F. BUCKLEY, NATIONAL REVIEW; DENNY'S; BROTHERHOOD of the SNAKE; LARRY KING, LARRY KING LIVE 9pm "CNN"; CHARLES E. "CHUCK" SCHUMER, SENATOR of NEW YORK; RASTAFARIAN NATIVES; SPENCER ABRAHAM, former SECRETARY of ENERGY; ROLLINGSTONE MAGAZINE; MONOGRAM BANK of GEORGIA d/b/a GE CAPITAL; GRACE JONES; NATIONAL ASSOCIATION for STOCK CAR AUTO RACING "NASCAR"; RAMZI AHMED YOUSEF; PLANET HOLLYWOOD; JOSEPH H. BOARDMAN, FEDERAL RAILROAD ADMINISTRATOR; MARSHALL BRUCE MATHERS 111, SHADY RECORDS INC a/k/a EMINEM; ULLUMINATI, founder ADAM WEISHAUPT; THE APOLLO THEATER; DAVID W. ANDERSON, ASSISTANT SECRETARY FOR INDIAN AFFAIRS; JASON SOCIETY; WU TANG CLAN, WU-WEAR INC; PHILIP PURCELL, CEO MORGAN STANLEY DEAN WITTER; NORDIC GODS; PRESIDENTAL EMERGENCY OPERATIONS CENTER "PEOC"; SCREEN ACTORS GUILD INC; R. JAMES NICHOLSON, SECRETARY of VETERANS AFFAIRS; NEW YORK STOCK EXCHANGE INC "NYSE"; THE DA VINCI CODE; MOORISH SCIENCE TEMPLE of AMERICA "MSTA"; SEARS TOWER; MIKE TYSON; NATIVE AMERICAN FISH SOCIETY; HOLOCAUST SURVIVORS; BYZANTINE REPUBLIC ARMY "BRA"; DENNIS HOPPER; MT. RUSHMORE; BARBARA WALTERS, ABC 20/20; FIRST PRESBYTERIAN CHURCH; GORDON R. SULLIVAN, former GENERAL/CHAIRMAN JOINT CHIEFS of STAFF; YELLOW CAB COMPANY; GREEK ORTHODOX ARCHDIOCESE of NORTH AMERICA; MICHAEL SAVAGE, SAVAGE NATION; DENNIS HASTERT, REPUBLICAN SPEAKER of HOUSE of REPRESENTATIVES; GREEN BAY'S LAMBEAU FIELD; SLOBODAN MILOSEVIC, former PRESIDENT of SERBIA; PIZZA HUT; KING JAMES BIBLE; SCOTT PETERSON; DEPARTMENT of HOUSING and URBAN DEVELOPMENT "HUD"; SMITHSONIAN INSTITUTE; ROBERT C. BONNER, COMMISSIONER UNITED STATES CUSTOM SERVICE; MING DYNASTY; RAY NAGIN, NEW ORLEANS MAYOR; BARRY BONDS; THOMAS J. RIDGE, former DIRECTOR of DEPARTMENT of HOMELAND SECURITY; JENNA BUSH, daughter of PRESIDENT of UNITED STATES; GANGS in HONG KONG; UNITED METHODIST CHURCH; EUROPEAN UNION; PORTER GOSS, DIRECTOR CENTRAL INTELLIGENCE AGENCY "CIA"; HARRAH'S LAS VEGAS INC; GRAND WIZARD of KU KLUX KLAN "KKK"; GENERAL MOTORS "GM"; CHRISTOPHER COX, CHAIRMAN SECURITES and EXCHANGE COMMISSION "SEC"; PROCTOR & GAMBLE; JEWISH SYNAGOGE'S; www.EBAY.com; KNIGHTS OF MALTA; AFL-CIO UNION; BOOKER T. WASHINGTON; NATIONAL HOCKEY LEAGUE "NHL" PLAYERS ASSOCIATION; DIANE SAWYER, co-anchor GOOD MORNING AMERICA ABC/WALT DISNEY CO; IMMIGRATION and NATURALIZATION SERVICE "INS"; VERN MINNI ME; STEVE JOBBS, CEO APPLE COMPUTERS INC; STATUE of LIBERTY; FIDEL CASTRO, PRESIDENT of CUBA; BRIAN L. ROBERTS, COMCAST CABLE CO; EARTH LIBERATION FRONT "ELF"; PHIL DONAHUE; MALCOLM X; KIM JONG 11, PRESIDENT of NORTH KOREA; GENEVA CONVENTION; LEE SCOTT, CEO WAL-MART. ARIZONA GAME and FISH COMMISSION; NELSON ROCKEFELLER; NATIONAL ASSOCIATION of REALTORS;

FORT KNOX; PHILADELPHIA EAGLES, 2005 ROSTER, including DONOVAN MCNABB; CHURCH OF SCIENTOLOGY; WORLD TRADE ORGANIZATION "WTO"; BURT REYNOLDS; INTERNET CORPORATION for ASSIGNED NAMES and NUMBERS "ICANN"; MICHAEL A. AQUINO, FOUNDER SANTANIC TEMPLE of SET; BILL O'REILLY, "THE O'REILLY FACTOR" FOX NEWS CORP; PUERTO RICAN NATIONALIST PARTY; WESTERN UNION FINANCIAL SERVICES; PAULA ABDUL; UNITED STATES HOLOCAUST MUSEUM; SISTER SOULJAH; SUHA ARAFAT, WIFE of late YASIR ARAFAT; REVEREND JESSIE JACKSON; HAMID KARZAI, PRESIDENT of AFGHANISTAN; CARNIVAL CRUISE LINES; THE WORLD COURT HAGUE; BEN N JERRY'S ICECREAM; JANET RENO, former ATTORNEY GENERAL; HOUSE of ROTHSCHILD; DAVID STERN, COMMISSIONER NATIONAL BASKETBALL ASSOCIATION "NBA"; INTERNATIONAL MONETARY FUND "IMF"; JIMMY DEAN SAUSAGE CO; YALE SKULL and BONES; SUMNER REDSTONE, CEO CBS/VIACOM; COMPUTER HACKERS and TELEPHONE PHREAKERS; MAYFLOWER MOVING CORP; CHEMICAL/ BIO SENSOR RESEARCH CENTER, ABERDEEN MARYLAND; WHOOPI GOLDBERG; VINCENTE FOX, PRESIDENT of MEXICO; PENNSYLVANIA LOTTERY COMMISSION; www.AMAZON.com; MICHAEL CHERTOFF, DIRECTOR DEPATMENT of HOMELAND SECURITY; CITY of NADI, FIJI ISLANDS; THE NEW YORK TIMES; AMERICAN EXPRESS credit card CORP; THE OLSEN TWINS; RAINBOW/PUSH COALITION; MOHAMMED ATTA, WORLD TRADE CENTER hijacker; LEAVENWORTH FEDERAL PRISON; MAX MAYFIELD, DIRECTOR NATIONAL WEATHER SERVICE; MICHAEL TIGAR, ATTORNEY of late TIMOTHY MCVEIGH; ROMAN EMPIRE; MERRIAM WEBSTERS DICTIONARY 10TH EDITION; PALESTINE LIBERATION ORGANIZATION "PLO"; MICHAEL H. ARMACOST, PRESIDENT of BROOKINGS INSTITUTE; KRAFT FOODS INC; JOHN FUND, EDITOR WALL ST. JOURNAL; unknown writers of NORTH AMERICAN FREE TRADE AGREEMENT "NAFTA"; DEMI MOORE; SMITH N WESSON; UNITED NEGRO COLLEGE FUND; EDWARD M. LIDDY, CHAIRMAN/CEO ALLSTATE INSURANCE CORP; WOLF BLITZER, "THE SITUATION ROOM" CNN NEWS; www.2600.com; METROPOLITAN TRANSIT AUTHORITY; RICHARD JEWEL; BLOODS and CRIPS of DETROIT; MICHAEL J. FOX; RICHARD S. FULD, CEO LEHMAN BROTHERS; VERIZON COMMUNICATIONS d/b/a "BELL ATLANTIC" d/b/a "GTE"; ANGELA MERKEL, PRESIDENT of GERMANY; THE ROSE BOWL; BEN YAHWEH; PEOPLE AGAINST TREATMENT of ANIMALS "PETA"; KENTUCKY FRIED CHICKEN; CITIGROUP INC; NATIONAL ACADEMY of SCIENCE'S INSTITUTE of MEDICINE; INDRA K. NOOYI, PRESIDENT of PEPSICO INC; VIRGINIA KINGS DOMINION; VANNA WHITE; ROBERT W. KAGAN, CARNEGIE ENDOW INTERNATIONAL PEACE; SUGAR RAY LEONARD; ROSS PEROT; HARLEY-DAVIDSON INC; INTERNATIONAL ISLAMIC RELIEF ORGANIZATION "IIRO"; HARLEY G. LAPPIN, DIRECTOR FEDERAL BUREAU of PRISONS "BOP"; PINK TRIANGLE COALITION; POW-MIA; CATHEDRAL CHURCH of the INTERCESSOR; BELLEVUE STATE HOSPITAL CENTER; www.FRAUDFEDERALRESERVE.com; SAMMY SOSA; ROBERT M. GATES, PRESIDENT TEXAS A & M; ARCHITECTURE of FREE MASONRY; BOBBY ACCORD, ADMINISTRATOR ANIMAL and HEALTH INSPECTION SERVICES; THE PILLSBURY COMPANY; REVOLUTIONARY ARMED FORCES of COLOMBIA "FARC"; ROSIE O'DONNELL; GEORGE P. SHULTZ, former SECRETARY of STATE, MOZART; SUNDANCE FILM FESTIVAL; U.S. CAPITOL POLICE; AARP, AMERICANS ASSOCIATION of RETIRED PERSONS; THE APPALACHIAN TRAIL; NOTRE DAME; JOHN KASICH, former CHAIRMAN HOUSE BUDGET COMMITTEE; JOEY BUTTAFUOCO; NATIONAL WILDLIFE REFUGE; NOSTRADAMUS; RICHARD THORNBURGH, former ATTORNEY GENERAL; LEANN RIMES; EVANGELICAL LUTHERAN CHURCH; DR. JAMES BILLINGTON, LIBRARY of CONGRESS; MARCO POLO; TERESA HEINTZ KERRY; NEGRO JUSTICE LEAGUE; THE EIFFEL TOWER; NEWT GINGRICH, former HOUSE SPEAKER; USA TODAY; G8 SUMMIT; ZACARIAS MOUSSAOUI; RINGLING BROS. and BARNUM & BAILEY CIRCUS; KENTUCKY MILITIA; LLOYD M. BENTSEN, former SECRETARY of TREASURY; JOHN WAYNE BOBBIT; PLYMOUTH ROCK; WKRP in CINCINNATI; ROYAL INSTITUTE for INTERNATIONAL AFFAIRS; ARAYAN BROTHERHOOD; JAMES G. ROCHE, SECRETARY of AIR FORCE; YAO MING; HARTSFIELD ATLANTA INTERNATIONAL AIRPORT; www.ANTISOCIAL.com; CHARLES DICKENS; ARLEN SPECTOR, SENATOR of PENNSYLVANIA, CHAIRMAN JUDICIARY COMMITTEE; LEANING TOWER of PISA; NATIONAL OCEANIC ATMOSPHERIC ADMINISTRATION "NOAA"; IRAQI BAATH REGIME; KEVIN BACON; UNITED STATES OLYMPIC COMMITTEE; HUMANE SOCIETY; GUERILLA'S in the MIST; DONNA E. SHALALA, former SECRETARY HEALTH and HUMAN SERVICES; FABIO; HOLY LAND FOUNDATION; ENCYCLOPEDIA BRITANNICA; BONO; CENTERS FOR DISEASE CONTROL "CDC"; HOME DEPOT; NATIONAL RIFLE ASSOCIATION "NRA"; GERALDO RIVERA; AMTRAK, NATIONAL RAIL PASSENGER CORP; NICCOLO MACHIAVELLI; AMERICAN PSYCHIATRIC ASSOCIATION; GARDEN of EDEN; BEN ROETHLISBERGER, PITTSBURGH STEELERS QUARTERBACK; UNIFICATION CHURCH; ANGLO-SAXONS ALLIANCE; UNITED STATES SECRET SERVICE; DOSTOEVSKY; THE INTERNATIONAL SPACE STATION, all parts manufacters; RUSSELL CROWE; ASSASSINS of SERBIAN PRIME MINISTER ZORAN DJINDJIC; MALL of AMERICA; EDWARD S. ROBINSON; COMMANDING OFFICER of USS GRAYBACK; HOME SHOPPING NETWORK "HSN"; JOHN DUPONT; ACE HARDWARE STORES; HENRY A. KISSINGER, former SECRETARY of STATE; PAUL REVERE; INDIANAPOLIS MOTOR SPEEDWAY;

DUNCAN DONUTS; RAND CORPORATION; MICHELANGELO; OLYMPIA J. SNOWE, SENATOR OF MAINE; AZTEC PYRAMIDS; BOY SCOUTS of AMERICA; DR. WILLIAM PIERCE, AUTHOR "THE TURNER DIARIES"; SIX FLAGS over ARLINGTON TEXAS; TALMUD; BETH HOLLOWAY TWITTY; INTERNATIONAL ATOMIC ENERGY AGENCY "IAEA"; JESSICA SIMPSON; DONALD E. GRAHAM, CEO WASHINGTON POST; VIAGRA; ANNE RICHARDS, former GOVERNOR of TEXAS; www.GINOROMANO.com; WILLIAM JEFFERSON CLINTON, FORMER PRESIDENT of THE UNITED STATES; MARION "SUGE" KNIGHT, DEATH ROW RECORDS; RIPLEY'S BELIEVE IT OR NOT; RANDY JOHNSON, NEW YORK YANKEES PITCHER; ANHEISER-BUSCH; PETER JENNINGS widow; PAUL WOLFOWITZ; MONTANA FREEMEN; PENNSYLVANIA TURNPIKE; ALCOHAL, TOBACCO, and FIREARMS "ATF"; JULIA ROBERTS; PUBLIC BROADCAST SYSTEM "PBS"; JEB BUSH, GOVERNOR of FLORIDA; JOHN BIRCH SOCIETY; SPRINT/NEXTEL; BOB VILA; HOOVER DAM; SANDY BERGER, former DIRECTOR NATIONAL SECURITY AGENCY "NSA"; TOLL BROTHERS builders; KILLINGTON VERMONT SKI RESORT; www.YAHOO.com; JOE GIBBS RACING; JENNIFER LOPEZ; NATIONAL PUBLIC RADIO "NPR"; TONYA HARDING; COMPTROLLER of CURRENCY; ADT SECURITY; HARRISON FORD; US DEPARTMENT of AGRICULTURE, MIKE JOHANNS; DELTA AIRLINES; PETE ROSE; SYMBIONESE LIBERATION ARMY "SLA"; SMALL BUSINESS ADMINISTRATION "SBA"; JOSEPH LIEBERMAN, SENATOR of CONNECTICUT; SYLVESTER STALLONE; KYOTO PROTOCOL; THE BOLIVIAN MAFIA; VIETNAM VETERANS of AMERICA; KENNETH STARR, former INDEPENDENT COUNCIL; SIMON and SCHUSTER; PATRICIA HEARST; ANTI-DEFAMATION LEAGUE; NELSON MANDELA, former PRESIDENT of SOUTH AFRICA; CHANDRA LEVY; CHURCH OF JESUS CHRIST LATTER DAY SAINTS; RUSH LIMBAUGH; AIRFORCE ONE; LOUIS FARRAKHAN, NATION OF ISLAM; NATIONAL MEDAL of ARTS; WEBSTER HUBBELL, MCDOUGAL'S, all WHITEWATER DEFENDANTS; THE WAFFLE HOUSE; GRAY DAVIS, former GOVERNOR of CALIFORNIA; BLACK PANTHER PARTY; GRAND CANYON-PARASHANT NATIONAL MONUMENT; LUCY LIU; BOB BARKER, HOST of PRICE IS RIGHT; FEDERALIST SOCIETY; ELIAN GONZALEZ; INTERNATIONAL CRIMINAL COURT "ICC"; DANNY GLOVER; NATIONAL ARCHIVES; DISNEY'S GRAND FLORIDIAN RESORT; JONATHAN JAY POLLARD, JEWISH SPY; RED GUERRILLA RESISTANCE; NEW JERSEY PORT AUTHORITY; CHRIS MATTHEWS, MSNBC "HARDBALL"; KWEISI MFUME, PRESIDENT "NAACP"; WENDY'S; M.C. HAMMER; RUDOLPH GIULIANI, former MAYOR of NEW YORK CITY; ISLAMIC MUSLIM BROTHERHOOD; DREW BARRYMORE; all NATIONAL ABORTION CLINICS; NEWSWEEK MAGAZINE; MADELEINE ALBRIGHT, former SECRETARY of STATE; LEE R. RAYMOND, CEO EXXON/MOBIL; LOUIS XV; HOLY GRAIL; MERCK PHARMACEUTICALS; SIR ELTON JOHN; PLANET of PLUTO; TRENT LOTT, SENATOR of MISSISSIPPI; HO CHI MINH CITY; COLONEL MUAMMAR GADDAFI, PRESIDENT of LIBYA; FRANK SINATRA JR; JOSEPH BIDEN , SENATOR of DELAWARE; LIL KIM, JUNIOR MAFIA BAD BOY RECORDS; I-95 "INTERSTATE" DEVELOPERS; MAKE a WISH FOUNDATION; THE VIRGIN MARY; US DEPARTMENT of INTERNAL AFFAIRS; RICHARD REID, SHOEBOMBER; JERRY LEWIS telethon; GOLDEN GATE BRIDGE; MONICA LEWINSKY; JOHN ASHCROFT, former ATTORNEY GENERAL; DENNIS RODMAN; CENTER for MEDICARE / MEDICAID SERVICES; J.K. ROWLING, author " HARRY POTTER"; JACKIE CHAN; NOELLE BUSH, JEB BUSH'S DAUGHTER; MISS CLEO; DAVID COULTER, former CEO BANK of AMERICA; CHECHEN REBELS; HUGGIES; COLIN POWELL, former SECRETARY of STATE; NINJA SAMURAI FIGHTERS; NATIONAL CENTER for MISSING & EXPLOITED CHILDREN; HAMAS; TAMMANY HALL; TREVOR SMITH d/b/a "BUSTA RHYMES" FLIP MODE RECORDS; www.EHARMONY.com; JEAN-BERTRAND ARISTIDE, former PRESIDENT of HAITI; HUBBLE SPACE TELESCOPE; JOSHUA BOLTEN, WHITE HOUSE BUDGET DIRECTOR; THE BOSTON GLOBE; THE NATIONAL GUARD and RESERVES; B'NAI B'RITH; OUTLAWS MOTORCYCLE GANG; JOHN MCCAIN, EX POW, SENATOR of ARIZONA; EQUAL OPPORTUNITY EMPLOYER "EOE"; MICHAEL MOORE; FORT BRAGG MILITARY BASE, all military ranks: PRIVATES,SERGEANTS,CAPTAINS,CORPORAL,GENERAL,MAJOR, ADMIRAL,COLONEL,LIEUTENANTS; JOHN WALTERS, WHITE HOUSE DRUG CZAR; WORLD WIDE WEB; CATHOLIC CHURCH, GAY CATHOLIC PRIESTS; BEN BERNANKE, FEDERAL RESERVE CHAIRMAN; ANTI-COMMUNIST MEMORBILA COLLECTION; ACADEMY AWARDS; FBI, BEHAVIORAL SCIENCES DIVISION; FRANCIS J. HARVEY, SECREATRY of ARMY; BAPTIST CHURCH; www.MEDIACONTROL.com; OPRAH WINFREY; AREA 69: ALIEN & UFO RESEARCH CENTER; SCOTT MCCLELLAN, WHITE HOUSE SPOKESMAN; DAVID DUKE; ENGINE #9, FIRE DEPARTMENT; FRANKLIN MINT; D.B. COOPER; LESTER CRAWFORD, US FOOD and DRUG ADMINISTRATION "FDA"; NAPOLEON; ORGANIZATION of PETROLEUM EXPORTING COUNTRIES "OPEC"; WICCAN WORSHIP; BRITISH SAS; GUANTANAMO BAY; THE DARRYL F. ZANCK INSTITUTE for MEDIA DOMINATION and TALMUDIC STUDIES; PIRATES COVE MINITURE GOLF COURSE; HANNIBAL LECTOR; COUNCIL of FOREIGN RELATIONS; RONALD MCDONALD CHARITIES; FODAY SANKOH, former PRESIDENT of SERRIE LEONE; BEN GURION AIRPORT; SANDRA BULLOCK; STATUE of FELIX DZERZHINSKY "IRON FELIX"; KATIE CURIC, CO-ANCHOR NBC'S TODAY SHOW; FEDERAL DEPOSIT INSURANCE CORPORATION "FDIC"; MOTLEY RICE; QUEEN RANIA of JORDAN; PHI BETA KAPPA; IRISH REPUBLICAN ARMY "IRA"; CHE GUEVARA; ALJAZEERA TELEVISION; BUMBLE BEE TUNA;

COPTIC ORTHODOX EGYPT CHURCH; JOHN BOEHNER, US HOUSE EDUCATION/WORKFORCE COMMITTEE CHAIRMAN; BIG BEND; SANDRA DAY O'CONNOR; DUN & BRADSTREET; BOB SAGET; SCOTLAND YARD; MOORISH SCIENCE TEMPLE of AMERICA; NCAA BASKETBALL; DRUG ENFORCEMENT AGENCY "DEA"; JAVELIN STRATEGY & RESEARCH; QODS FORCE (JERUSALEM FORCE); BOSTON MARKET; www.backstreetboys.com; HIZBALLAH; LAWRENCE LIVERMORE NATIONAL LABORATORY; RUSSIAN KGB; COLOSSIANS FIRST CENTURY PARALLELS; TERI HATCHER; GLORIA ARROYO, PRESIDENT of PHILIPPINES; TROJAN HORSE; RANDOM HOUSE PUBLISHING; GREAT WALL of CHINA; DEPARTMENT of JUSTICE "DOJ"; PERKINS; GENERAL OMAR TORRIJOS, FORMER PANAMA PRESIDENT; JEFF FORT, leader EL RUKN; DYNASTY 7; NATIONAL RECONNAISSANCE OFFICE "NRO"; GEORGE CLOONEY: JOSE MARTI AIRPORT, HAVANNA CUBA; KORAN; ASHANTI GOLDFIELDS; CLUB of ROME; NATO; CHARLES SCHWAB; KOREAN NATIONAL INTELLIGENCE SERVICE "NIS"; ANNE MULCAHY, CEO XEROX; KIRIAT; CONGRESS on RACIAL EQUALITY "CORE"; INTERPOL; KORYO DYNASTY; KILLERS of PRINCESS DIANA & DODI; WU YI, VICE PREMIER of CHINA; www.EXPEDIA.com; THE 48TH ANNUAL GRAMMY AWARDS; BRITISH MI5; FEDERAL RESERVE WIRE TRANSFER NETWORK "FEDWIRE"; POLYTHEISTS INTERNATIONAL; FEDERICO PENA, former SECRETARY of TRANSPORTATION; ABU SAYAFF; MARIAH CAREY; LONDON'S NATURAL HISTORY MUSEUM; COMMANDER of UNITED STATES COAST GUARD; TAOIST CREATURES; FINANCIAL CRIMES ENFORCEMENT NETWORK "FINCEN"; EGYPTIAN GAMA'AT; CHOICEPOINT; PELER BIJUR, CEO of TEXACO, BERLIN WALL DEMOLITION CO; DICK DEGUERIN; CRYPTOGRAPH ELICITATION CENTER "CEC"; GUY RITCHIE; THE SUPREME COURT; BOUSTROS GHALI, former UN SECRETARY GENERAL; GLAXO SMITH KLINE; FARAH AIDEED, SOMALI WARLORD; KIEFER SUTHERLAND; NEW REPUBLIC MAGAZINE; www.BOP.gov; ASPEN INSTITUTE; BURGER KING; FEDERAL BUREAU of INVESTIGATION "FBI", TINA TURNER; PATRIOTIC UNION of KURDISTAN "PUK"; DISNEY'S TYPHOON LAGOON; BUNDESKRIMINALAND, GERMAN FEDERAL POLICE; HEGELIAN PRINCIPLE; SHAMIL BASSAYEU; GORDON R. ENGLAND, SECRETARY of NAVY; PSYCHOLOGY SOCIALISM; MINNESOTA VIKINGS; MICHAEL V. HAYDEN, DIRECTOR NATIONAL SECURITY AGENCY "NSA"; SOUTHWEST AIRLINES; GENE HACKMAN; GOTHIC CELTIC INC; CAESERS PALACE; PENTAGON; BROOKLIN BRIDGE; KING of PRUSSIA MALL; TONY BLAIR, PRIME MINISTER of GREAT BRITAIN; COMMONWEALTH NATIONAL BANK; AL-SUGAYR AZMI, former HEAD of FATAH; LOS ANGELES POLICE DEPARTMENT; ALBERTO R GONZALES, UNITED STATES ATTORNEY GENERAL; FUBU CLOTHING LINE; MARTIN S. FELDSTEIN, HARVARD UNIVERSITY; BRITISH ROUND TABLE; GEORGE HERBERT WALKER BUSH, former PRESIDENT of UNITED STATES; MICHAEL DELL, CEO DELL COMPUTERS; BILLY BLANKS; MICHAEL IRVIN; LIGHT TECHNOLOGY PUBLISHING; CHUBBY CHECKER; DONALD B. ENSENAT, CHIEF OF PROTOCOL; MULTIPLE SCLEROSIS SOCIETY; CARDINAL BERNARD LAW; USS COLE; EASTER SEALS; GRAND DUCHY of LUXEMBOURG; PGA GOLF; SILVIO BERLUSCONI, PREMIER of ITALY; DENNIS KOZLOWSKI; BUCKINGHAM PALACE; VALERIE PLAME; BOYS & GIRLS CLUBS of AMERICA; ZEUS; GEORGE A. OMAS, POSTAL RATE COMMISSION; AMERICAN KENNEL CLUB; SUPER 8 MOTELS; DAVID FREUDENTHAL, GOVERNOR of WYOMING; CHERNOBYL NUCLEAR POWER PLANT; PFC. LYNNDIE ENGLAND; MADISON SQUARE GARDEN; SPAIN BASQUE "ETA"; JUSTIN TIMBERLAKE; JOHN HANCOCK FINANCIAL SERVICES; TIN CAN SAILORS; BILL JANKLOW, former HOUSE REP. of SOUTH DAKOTA; EMEKA OKAFOR; PARMALAT; KENTUCKY DERBY; GARY RIDGWAY; WORLD ANTI-DOPING AGENCY; HOWARD DEAN, former GOVERNOR of VERMONT; THE COLOSSUS of RHODES; BETTY CROCKER; LIBERTY BELL; THEODORE KACZYNSKI; US CENSUS BUREAU; BARCLAY'S PLC UK; ANDREW H. CARD, WHITE HOUSE CHIEF of STAFF; WEIRD AL YANKOVIC; BERNARD EBBERS, former CEO WORLD COM; MOKTADA AL-SADR, SHIITE CLERIC; GAY PRIDE PARADE; MARGARET THATCHER, former PRIME MINISTER of GREAT BRITAIN, BETTER BUSINESS BUREAU; LLOYDS of LONDON; WARSAW PACT; BARACK OBAMA, SENATOR of ILLINOIS; FORT MCHENRY TUNNEL; JACK KEVORKIAN; HANS BLIX, former UN WEAPONS INSPECTOR; THE DOOBIE BROTHERS; HOLY QURAN; BARBARA POPE, SECRETARY of CIVIL RIGHTS; ALZHEIMER'S ASSOCIATION; BENINGO G. REYNA, US MARSHALS SERVICE; WEIGHT WATCHERS; HU JINTAO, PRESIDENT PEOPLES REPUBLIC of CHINA; CALIFORNIA INSTITUTE of TECHNOLOGY; EMILIO ESTEVEZ; LACKLAND AIRFORCE BASE; MENNONITE CHURCH; PAT ROBERTS, SENATOR of KANSAS; CROWN PRINCE ALIOS, PRINCIPALITY of LIECHTENSTEIN; YMCA; IRAQI NATIONAL CONGRESS; www.PAYNOTAXES.com; GERHARD SCHROEDER, former CHANCELLOR of GERMANY; KEVIN MITNICK; CANADA'S LIBERAL PARTY; KEN JENNINGS, JEOPARDY CHAMPION; RUSSIAN FEDERATION 89; NATIONAL SECURITY COUNCIL "NSC"; AL PACINO; SULTANATE of OMAN; FOLGER SHAKESPERE LIBRARY; MEL GIBSON; JACQUES CHIRAC, PRESIDENT of FRANCE; MARTHA STEWART, LIVING OMNIMEDIA INC; MOUNT VERNON; DEPRESSION and BIPOLAR SUPPORT ALLIANCE; MBNA CORP; LADY BIRD JOHNSON WILD FLOWER CENTER; SOCIAL WORKERS PARTY "SWP"; NOBEL PEACE PRIZE, LA-Z-BOY; AMERICANS VERTERANS of WORLD WAR 11; NEW YORK MERCANTILE EXCHANGE; THE GENERAL ASSEMBLY; QUAKER OATS; CHARLES LOUIS KINCANNON; CONGOLESE ARMY; CHARLES DE GAULLE PARIS AIRPORT; SKITTLES CANDY; ARNOLD SCHWARZENEGGER: DEFENDANTS,

COMPLAINT

"NEW WORLD ORDER AGAINST MANKIND"

This is a complaint under 42 U.S.C §§ 1983, civil rights violation by the Constitution and laws of the United States; and Federal Tort claims inflicted by that include, but not limited to: 18 U.S.C. §§ 2339,2332 TERRORISM, 18 U.S.C. §§ 1111 MURDER, 18 U.S.C. §§ 2381 TREASON, 18 U.S.C. §§ 1031 MAJOR FRAUD, 18 U.S.C. §§ 878 EXTORTION, 18 U.S.C. §§ 1951,1961 RACKETEERING, 18 U.S.C. §§ 2340 TORTURE, 18 U.S.C. §§ 241 CIVIL RIGHTS, 18 U.S.C §§ 831 ESPIONAGE, 18 U.S.C §§ 111 ASSAULT, 18 U.S.C. §§ 371 CONSPIRACY, 18 U.S.C. §§ 1091 GENOCIDE, 18 U.S.C. §§ 2441 WAR CRIMES, 18 U.S.C §§ 831 EXPLOSIVES, 18 U.S.C. §§ 1501 OBSTRUCTION OF JUSTICE, 18 U.S.C. §§ 1651 PIRACY, 18 U.S.C §§ 81 ARSON, 18 U.S.C. §§ 2151 SABOTAGE, 18 U.S.C. §§ 1621 PERJURY, 18 U.S.C §§ 521 CRIMINAL STREET GANGS, 18 U.S.C. §§ 175 BIOLOGICAL WEAPONS, 18 U.S.C §§ 1591 SEX TRAFFICKING, 18 U.S.C. §§ 152 CONCEALMENT,FALSE OATHS,BRIBERY, 18 U.S.C. §§ 2101 RIOTS, 18 U.S.C. §§ 1581 SLAVERY, 18 U.S.C §§ 2111 ROBBERY, 18 U.S.C. §§ 1361 MALICIOUS MISCHIEF, 18 U.S.C. §§ 470 COUNTERFEITING, 18 U.S. C. §§ 2231 SEARCH AND SEIZURES, 18 U.S.C. §§ 41 INJURY TO WILDLIFE; 18 U.S.C. §§ 2241 SEX ABUSE/RAPE, 18 U.S.C. §§ 1460 OBSCENITY, 18 U.S.C §§ 1201 KID-NAPPING, 18 U.S.C. §§ 2261 STALKING, 18 U.S.C. §§ 1261 LIQUOR TRAFFICKING, IDENTITY THEFT, PSYCHIATRIC TRAUMA, FALSE INFORMATION, INVASION, THREATS TO COMMIT VIOLENT ACTS, MALPRACTICES, AGGRAVATIONS, NUISANCES, ENTRAPMENTS, MIND MANIPULATION, BRUTALITY, PERSECUTIONS, NEGLIGENCE, ELECTRONIC WIRETAPPING, AND POISONING.

Comes now the Plaintiff Jonathan Lee., Riches©, in pro-se, moves this Honorable Court to issue an Order for all Defendant's named in this suit to give a response. Moves this Honorable Court to list all Defendant's in complaint each and separate as shown, not ect. all. As the Plaintiff is claiming that his Federal & State Constitution Rights are being violated under the 1st, 2nd, 4th, 5th, 6th, 8th, 13th, and 14th amendment of the Constitution. Relief requested, Plaintiff seeks 379,111,339,000,000.00 Trillion dollars backed by gold or silver delivered by United Parcel Service "UPS" to Federal correctional Institution Williamsburg, Salters South Carolina, collectively from all Defendants.

COUNT 1

Vast conspiracy through Defendant's for New World Order forcing the Uniform Commercial Code "UCC" on my life. False pretences created the ALL CAPS of my flesh and blood name forcing me to do business with the DE FACTO / ENS LEGIS UNITED STATES GOVERNMENT. The Defendant's through subliminal messaging and RFID on star chips, combined with daily life technology suckers me into contract. The federal Reserve Bank is unconstitutional, federal reserve notes (fiat money) are backed by no substance except the American Citizens "promise". The Defendants are spreading this concept globally, preventing anyone from leaving this planet. Flights from travel agencies are suspended according to TRAVELOCITY.com.

COUNT 2

George Bush is a time traveler, conspired with Duke of Normandy at Battle of Hastings 1066 A.D. to pervert the English Dictonary and Law. Admiral / Maritime Jurisdiction is hearing my complaint. The american flag is M.I.A. held hostage at FEMA camps.

COUNT 3

George W. Bush is the grand Iman of voodoo witch doctors turning humans to animals, sometimes plants. April 14Th, 2001 was witnessed seen together with United Nations Secreatry General Kofi Annan at a Falls Church Virginia smorgasbord, discussing top secret protocol, and Social Security as a Ponzi Scam.

COUNT 4

Trading with Enemy Act of October 6th, 1917, yet George W. Bush and Defendants secretly sell inmates DNA on the international stock market including, but not limited to: HITLER'S SOCIALIST PARTY, GUERILLA ASIAN MOVEMENT, and on 3 occations the NIGERIAN JUNJAWEED'S.

COUNT 5

Defendant's were involved with FCI WILLIAMSBURG'S construction, failing to build an ANTI- UFO defense system, releasing staph infection in the water system, hiring Robotic correctional guards.

COUNT6

The 14TH amendment of the Constitution was not ratified properly. Myself was not allowed a vote. Mysterious supernatural creatures drinking YOOHOO. Condi Rice is a NASA created experiment, spreading false democracy. Secret black / white race war.

COUNT 7

HOUSE JOINT RESOLUTION 192 of June 5TH, 1933. Defendant's planned Elizabeth Smarts kidnapping. George W. Bush intercepted on Federal Wiretap, on the final stages of a secret Government weather making machine.

COUNT 8

People acted separately and together to accomplish the following:

* March 4TH, 2003- George W. Bush stole my Identity

* July 22ND, 2002- George W. Bush joined alliance with AL-Qaeda

* May 10TH, 2000- covert prostitution at local utility companies

* October 18TH, 2001- radiation released by United Airline Pilots

* January 9TH, 2004- hypnotherapists who advertise in newspapers

* December 25TH, 2002- price gouging citizens

Plaintiff's back was injured. Was forced fed. Security and Exchanges commission stole PLaintiff's money. 2 ingrown toe nails. Missing americans at college frat houses. Plaintiff seeks relief in monetary amount set at beginning complaint also granting this Honorable Court to impose a restraining order against George W. Bush. Please also include Restraing order against Airforce one.

Jonathan Lee, Riches©

UNITED STATES DISTRICT COURT
SOUTHERN DISTRICT OF TEXAS
HOUSTON DIVISION

Jonathan Lee., Riches(c) a/k/a §
"Secured Party", §
Plaintiff § CRIMINAL NUMBER: H-03-90-02
§
§
VS. §
§
UNITED STATES OF AMERICA, AUSA JAY §
HILEMAN, FBI SPECIAL AGENT SHAUNA §
A. DUNLAP, §
DEFENDANT'S §
§

"MOTION FOR PRELIMINARY INJUNCTION"
"MOTION FOR TEMPORARY RESTRAINING ORDER"

COMES NOW the Plaintiff, Jonathan Lee., Riches(c) a/k/a "Secured Party", in pro-se, Moves this Honorable Chief Judge to issue a temporary restraining order "TRO" and Preliminary injunction against Federal District Judge Melinda Harmon and her April 19th, 2006 Order against Plaintiff in having his forfeited property donated to Goodwill Industries, due to numerous Conflicts of interest between Melinda Harmon, Goodwill Industries, and the Government. As Plaintiff's Constitutional rights are still being violated under the 1st, 4th, 5th, 8th, 6th and 14th Amendment.

This Honorable Court has Jurisdiction because Plaintiff's criminal Case referenced above is from the Southern District of Texas in Houston, and this Court handled Plaintiff's Motion for return of Property.

PRELIMINAY INJUNCTION

Under Rule 65(a), Plaintiff asks this Honorable Chief Judge for a Preliminary Injunction against Melinda Harmon and her April 19th, 2006 Order against Plaintiff's property being forfeited to Goodwill Industries for the following reasons;

PLAINTIFF'S APPEAL AND DUE PROCESS VIOLATIONS

Plaintiff is currently appealing Melinda Harmon's April 19th, 2006 order forfeiting Personal property to goodwill Industries. Plaintiff recieved notice of that April 19th, 2006 Order for the first time June 19th, 2006, violated Plaintiff's 5th amendment right to due process. This first time notice was enclosed in a brown envelope post marked June 13th, 2006. (exhibit 3). This Clerk of Court Neglected to notify Plaintiff in a proper matter according to Law, as the Courts never Certified any Mail to Plaintiff to ensure he would recieve that April 19th, 2006 in a timely matter. This neglect could of been avoided if Plaintiff recieved proper notice. Many theories now stand in Plaintiff not recieving the April 19th, 2006 Order; the Clerk of Court never sent Plaintiff proper Notification due to a personal bias and prejudice with Plaintiff having a financial interest with Plaintiff's victims, or FCI WILLIAMSBURG facility never gave Plaintiff his mail, or the Clerk of Court sent notification, but due to it not being Certifed through the Post Office, the Mail got lost. Plaintiff does not know the reason why he did not get this April 19th, 2006 Order in a timely fashion. This is a due process violation. The Plaintiff asks this Honorable Court for a Preliminary injunction and Temporary restraining order against Melinda Harmon and her April 19th, 2006 Order, this will ensure Plaintiff due process while he appeals this April 19th, 2006 Order to the appeals and/or Supreme Court, the damages in Plaintiff losing his propery cannot be compensated in Monetary damages. Plaintiff also asks for A Preliminay Injunction and Temporary restraining order against Goodwill Industries in recieving Plaintiff's property as Plaintiff is currently appealing that Order.

41(g)

The substantial likelihood of success on the merits with a Preliminary Injunction and Temporary restraining order the Plaintiff is asking, not only because the Plaintiff is appealing, but Numerous violations under 41(g).

Under 41(g)- Motion must be filed in the district where the property was seized. Plaintiff's property was seized at his residence at 2521 Morning Glory Court, Holiday florida 34691, in the Middle District of Florida. This Court never had Jurisdiction on the Motion Plaintiff filed, as he mistakenly filed a 41(g) motion in the wrong venue.

UNITED AIRLINES INC V. WIENER 335 F 2d 379 (1967)- chooses wrong venue in first instance, he should not be deprived of to correct his mistake at a later date.

Plaintiff filed "Motion to dismiss for improper venue", "motion to transfer to cure want of Jurisdiction", and "motion for change of venue hearing" with this Court because of the wrong venue under 41(g) and Plaintiff re-filed a new 41(g) Motion for return of property in the Middle District of Florida where his property was taken.

ARREDONDO V. MOSER, LEXUS 22532 (5th)- 1997 arrest, property was seized at his place of business in Grand Prairie Texas on a arrest Warrant from U.S. District Court Western District of Tennessee. April 24, 2002, filed a 41(g) Motion with the Western District of Tennessee. June 4th, 2002, Court denied because under 41(g) such a Motion may only be filed in the District where property was Seized.

This Court never had Jurisdiction over Plaintiff's Property return Motion under 41(g) that he filed. Melinda Harmon's April 19th, 2006 Order is being appealed, and this Court needs to issue a Preliminary Injunction and Temporary restraining Order as Plaintiff will suffer serious harm later explained in this Motion.

violation of unlawful search and seizure

The Government violated Plaintiff's 4th amendment right to illegal search and seizure. Plaintiff never recieved any of the Warrants; Feb 25th, Feb 26th, Feb 27th, March 7th, March 13th, 2003. The Government failed to show or produce copies of Warrant's to Plaintiff. This Due Process and Constitutional right was in violation as the Government performed unlawful search and seizure, unlawful trespass, and wrongful forfeiture. This Court has denied Plaintiff's request for Discovery compelling the Government to produce to Plaintiff; all Warrant's at his residence, Affidavits of what property was taken on each day Plaintiff's home was searched, list of property taken, any statements made to FbI agents said in reference to taken property, copy of original arrest complaint, violating under BRADY V. MARYLAND, as the Government failed disclose exculpatory evidence. This Court never had jurisdiction in ruling on Plaintiff's property return Motion, as Plaintiff filed his 41(g) in the Middle District of Florida. Exhibit 8 clearly says at the top that it does not reach the threshold for forfeiture, the forfeiture under fed rule crim pro 32.2 should of been mentioned in indictment, plea bargin, or at time of sentencing, neither happened.

violation of 1st amendment

Plaintiff's is suffering a 1st amendment violation as theMelinda Harmon ruled that Property be forfeitured, as Plaintiff spoke out that she should of recused herself from any Criminal forfeiture proceedings under 28 USC §455 (a), (b), (c), D(4), B(4), B(5), "financial Interest" and "bias and prejudice". Supreme Court case LILJEBERG V. HEALTH SERVICES. Plaintiff asked the Courts for Melinda Harmon's recusal, but Melinda Harmon denied her own recusal Motion. This 1st amendment violation is violating freedom of speach as Plaintiff is addressing a serious issue of conflcits of interest between Melinda Harmon/ her family within the 3rd degree and Plaintiff's victims on his criminal case. This Conflict of interest also showed bias in Mr. Riches not recieving due process in proper Notification on Harmon's April 19th, 2006 Order, and knowing that Plaintiff filed his 41(g) in the wrong jurisdiction, but ruling that the property can be forfeitured anyway, this is a total "miscarriage of justice". A preliminary injuction and temporary restraining order must be imposed as Plaintiff appeals Harmon's conflicts of interest, and appeals his 41(g) filed in the wrong venue.

FAILURE TO GRANT THE INJUNCTION WILL RESULT IN IRREPARABLE INJURY

Plaintiff will suffer irreparable injury if his forfeiture property goes to goodwill Industries. Threatned damages cannot be compensated in Monetary damages. The list of items in exhibit 8 is Plaintiff's personal property. Computers; Apple g4, toshiba, tiger systemax were all personal computers that Plaintiff used. Plaintiff's personal identity, financial records, personal pictures, private information is stored in each computers hard drives and personal memory. By giving these Computers to Goodwill industries endangers the Plaintiff's personal information falling into 3rd parties hands. As once Goodwill Industires accepts Plaintiff's property, then gives Plaintiff's property/or sells it to someone else, who can in return, look in the hard drives, memory, or computer history, and discover personal information on Plaintiff, Plaintiff's family, that can then be used in a crime. Identity theft, fraud. etc. This is a total invasion of privacy . Pictures in the Computers, and digital camera's memory that Plaintiff does not want disclosed to anyone. This threatened injury outweighs any damage that the injunction may cause the opposing party, and the injunction will not disserve the public interest. Plaintiff does not want his personal banking and home addresses, and private telephone numbers stored in these computers and camera's in the wrong peoples hands while Plaintiff appeals his property return 41(g) Motion, and files it in the correct venue. This will harm Plaintiff. ALLIED MARKETING GROUP, INC V. CDL MARKETING, INC 878 F.2d 806 (5th 1989), and AFFILIATED PROF'L HOME HEALTH CARE AGENCY V. SHALALA 164 F. 3d 282 (5th 1999). Cell Phones in Exhibit 8 also contain memory and address books of personal family and associates of Plaintiff that Plaintiff does not want in the wrong hands while Plaintiff appeals hsi 41(g) Motion.

GOODWILL INDUSTRIES

Conflicts of interest between Goodwill Industries and Plaintiff's victims on his Criminal case. Both had financial Interests with Plaintiff's victims.

Even through the Plaintiff states that his personal property was not bought or recieved fraudulently, the Government claims the Property was bought with fraudulent credit cards. The Judge ruled April 19th, 2006 on the Government's claim, and now Plaintiff's property is to be forfeitured to goodwill industries;

under 18 USC § 2315 Goodwill industries should be charged with stolen property and recieving stolen property, as the Government is donating Stolen property to Goodwill Industries, with Goodwill Industires knowing the property is stolen.

Goodwill industries is also involved with illegal contributions to the Government, in exchange for forfeiture property, Not only with Plaintiff's property, but other peoples property past and present. This illegal practice must be looked into, and Plaintiff is entitled to any relief under the whistle blowing act.

RELIEF

For all the mention reasons above Plaintiff needs a restraining order and preliminary injunction. Plaintiff has showed all 4 factors, allied supra, and the likehood that a preliminary injunction will prevail. under 65(a), and 65(b), Plaintiff is also entitled to a hearing and requests a hearing on this Motion. Plaintiff also summitts an Affidavit on these issues. Prays this Honorable Court gives him relief.

JONATHAN LEE RICHES #40948-018
FCI WILLIAMSBURG
P.O. BOX 340
SALTERS, SOUTH CAROLINA 29590

respectfully,

(signature)

Jonathan Lee., Riches[(c)]
U.C.C. 1-308

Affiant hereby affirms and states the following facts and certifies that he is of lawful age, competent to testify to the matters contain herein, from first hand Personal Knowledge

Comes Now Jonathan Lee., Riches© who now states as follows;

I'm filing a Preliminary Injunction and temporary Restraing order against Melinda Harmon and the forfeiture of my property to goodwill Industries. I will suffer serious harm if my personal property gets in the hands of Goodwill or who ever they give/sell it to as personal private information is stored in the harddrives and memories. I'm appealing Harmons April 19th, 2006 ruling, and I filed a 41(g) motion in the correct venue of middle district of Florida.

2) Melinda Harmon has a financial interest with my victims on my criminal case and should of recused herself on my property relin motion. Goodwill industries also has a financial interest with my victims, and should not recieve that property. Melinda Harmon should recuse herself on this preliminary Injunction and Restraing order because of conflicts of interest

3) My property is not stolen or bought with credit cards, the Government says it is. The Government then wants to give stolen Property to Goodwill Industries. The CEO of Goodwill must be notified, and goodwill must be investigated for the practice of recieving stolen property

The Affiant Attests and Affirms that the facts contain herein are true, correct, complete, and are Not misleading in any material respect, and Based on Personal Knowledge

"I declare under Penalty or Perjury that the foregiving is true and Correct"

Jonathan Lee, Riches©
June 24th, 2006

IN THE UNITED STATES DISTRICT COURT
DISTRICT OF NEW HAMPSHIRE

Jonathan Lee, Riches© A/K/A
"Secured Party",
Plaintiff

VS.

CASE NO: 07-jp-212

Jewish Mossad;
Central Intelligence Agency "CIA";
Larry King Live,

Defendants

Complaint
"THE HIJACKING OF AMERICA"

This is a complaint under 42 U.S.C 1983, civil rights violation by the constitution and laws of the United States, and Federal Tort claims inflicted by that include, but not limited to: Kidnapping, extortion, Injury to wildlife, Liquor Trafficking, Identity theft, Persecutions, Electronic wire tapping

Comes Now the Plaintiff Jonathan Lee, Riches©, in Pro-se, moves this honorable court to issue an order for all Defendants named in this suit to give a response. As Plaintiff is claiming that his Federal and State constitutional rights are being violated under the 1st, 2nd, 4th, 5th, 6th, 8th, 13th, and 14th amendments. Plaintiff moves this honorable court to issue a TRO restraining order against Defendants. Plaintiff seek 211,429,399,000,000.00 Trillion dollars backed by gold and silver delivered by United States Postal Service to Federal Correctional Institution Williamsburg, Salters S.C., collectively from Defendants

Count 1

Defendants are in a vast conspiracy to Hijack my torso, 3 toes, and my constitutional rights and ship them to a secret headquarters in Concord New Hampshire.

Count 2

Jewish Mossad told me personally on April 20th, 2007 that they are going to hang me to a cross next to Jesus Christ

Count 3

Larry King Live is a voodoo witch doctor who stole my identity on Feb 25th 2003 and purchased lead paint, chips ahoy, Planters peanuts and zip lock bags under my identity, Distributed them to the CIA to microwave test my DNA

Count 4

The CIA on Jan 4th, 2006 plead allegience to Al-qaeda and conspired with the Uniform commercial code "U.C.C." to steal my Strawman Identity

Count 5

FCI Williamsburg hired Robotic guards financed through the Mossad and Capital 1 banking.

Covert prostitution, grave yard stealing, garage sale theft operation

Count 6

Defendants are involved with Trading with the Enemy Act by donating my Art work to N. Korea and Burma in exchange for weapons being shipped to Sudan's Janjaweed next door to Chad

Count 7

Defendants inserted micro chips and are dashing my hopes

Plaintiff respectfully acts this court for relief and to order a restraining order against Defendants and NASA.

Submitted

Jonathan Lee, Ricks

Jonathan Lee, Riches
#40948-018
FCI Williamsburg
P.O. Box 340
Salters, SC 29590

Due to restrictions on typewriters, this suit was handwritten

RECEIVED EASTERN DISTRICT OF ARKANSAS
MAIL ROOM
AUG 28 2007
U.S. DISTRICT COURT
E. DIST. OF ARKANSAS

FILED
U.S. DISTRICT COURT
EASTERN DISTRICT ARKANSAS
AUG 28 2007
JAMES W. McCORMACK, CLERK
By: _____ /DEP CLERK

Jonathan Lee Riches © d/b/a
Rockefeller Riches,
Plaintiff

CIVIL NO 4:07CV00780 SWW/JTR

V.

WALMART STORES INC,

DEFENDANTS

_____ assigned to _____ Wright
and to _____ J. _____ Ray

CIVIL COMPLAINT
"WALMART SCANDAL"

Plaintiff, who is deaf and blind, diagnosed with terminal cancer brings this Civil Suit against Walmart Stores pursuant to violation of the Americans with Disability Act (ADA) 42 USC 12101, violation of the Rehabilitation Act 29 USC 701, violation of the Age discrimination in Employment act of 1967, Title VII of the Civil Rights act of 1964 42 USC 2000, violations of State Labor codes and intentional infliction of emotional distress.

Comes now the Plaintiff, Jonathan Lee Riches © d/b/a Rockefeller Riches, in pro.se, Moves this Honorable Court to issue an order for Defendants named in this suit to respond. Plaintiff also seeks compensatory and punitive damages in the amount of $5,000,000.00 million against Defendants. Plaintiff moves for a Jury trial. Plaintiff moves to request Motion for Counsel. Plaintiff prays for relief.

Background

Plaintiff, who is deaf and blind, diagnosed with terminal cancer is a former Boys Scout of America den leader, former singer in the Church Choir, Philanthropist, and humanitarian aid was hired by Walmart Stores, INC

On May 4, 2003 under a disability internship program, I was under the care and supervision of Walmart management and supervisors. The very first day I worked for Walmart, my life has become a living nightmare. Managers picked on me. I was poked at, spit on my Walmart cashiers. Walmart Janitors would trip me with their mop handle. I was the laughing stock of Walmart. Walmart Managers would perform evil pranks on me. I remember on May 26, 2003 I was told to cut vegetables in the deli section, Managers knowing I can't see. Afterward, supervisors made me collect shopping carts in the parking lot. June 4, 2003, in Isle 3 (toys section) I was cleaning a Lego spill, fellow employee's blew a clown horn in my ear. Walmart does not provide the blind with Braille. On June 17, 2003 Walmart used my disability to solicit donations. I was forced to sit up front in a greeting chair with a donation cup. This was against my will, as Walmart management strapped and shackled me to the chair. Every morning when I reported to work I could not see the time clock to punch in. Walmart only gave me pay for 3 hr work weeks when in fact I would work 7 days a week from 7am to 7pm. This amounted to 84 hour weeks, but Walmart Management only paid me for 21 hours each week. I cashed my work check in the store, and every employee who cashed my check took my money. Walmart Employee's would send me anonymous notes in Braille calling me "the Elephant man", "Hellen Keller wannabe". Walmart forces employees to sign a "vow of secrecy" contract. Walmart does not want the world to know they hire Latin and Mexican underage illegals and harbor them in the back warehouse. These illegals are forced into prostitution. Walmart has a hidden room in back of the Nail department with a electric chair for workers who don't cooperate. On July 10, 2003, Walmart managers gave all the employees cocaine to enhance performance. Walmart hires convicted child molesters to drive their shipping tractor trailers. Walmart Managers at every United States location has been skimming the books to avoid IRS taxes. Walmart sells the public tainted dog food from China. Walmart Cashers serve liquor to minors.

1

On September 3, 2003, I was told by Walmart managers that I was fired because I'm blind. I was called "a dumb blind bat" and told I look like one of the "three blind mice". Walmart management told me "we don't need you deaf idiots working for us". Another said "see your way out of here". I also did not recieve back pay for 3 weeks.

CONCLUSION

Walmart is prejudice against any worker with a disability. I've suffered serious trauma since I worked at walmart. Walmart made my life a nightmare. Walmart lies in their commercials. Walmart treats elderly employee's even worse. I will never work for walmart again. I will never shop at walmart in my life. Plaintiff prays for relief and an injunction against walmarts illegal acts.

Respectfully submitted

Jonathan Lee Riches ©
Jonathan Lee Riches ©
U.C.C. 1-308

Jonathan Lee Riches ©
#40948-018
FCI Williamsburg
P.O. Box 340
Salters, SC 29590
(843) 387-9400

DISTRICT OF DELAWARE

Jonathan Lee Riches©,
Plaintiff   CIVIL NO: 07-538-

V.

SENATOR LARRY CRAIG (R) IDAHO;
REP. MARK FOLEY (R) FLORIDA;
SENATOR DAVID VITTER (R) LOUISIANA;
REP. BARNEY FRANK (D) MASSACHUSETTS;
ROMAN CATHOLIC PRIESTS;
KOBE BRYANT;
R KELLY;
WARREN JEFFS;
DUKE LACROSSE PLAYERS;
MICHAEL JACKSON;
JAMES McGREEVY FORMER NEW JERSEY GOVERNOR;
WILLIAM JEFFERSON CLINTON,
DEFENDANTS

FILED SEP -7 2007 U.S. DISTRICT COURT DISTRICT OF DELAWARE
PD scanned no IFP

Civil complaint

"PERVERTING AMERICA"

"TRO TEMPORARY RESTRAINING ORDER"

"PRELIMINARY INJUNCTION"

Comes now the Plaintiff, Jonathan Lee Riches©, in pro-se, moves this Honorable court to issue an order for Defendants named in this suit to respond. This suit is civil rights and liberties that Defendants committed against me. Also crimes of sexual harassment, sodomy of my mind, mental torture, mistrust, breaking my heart, embarrassment, deceit, and Fraud. Plaintiff also moves this Honorable court to issue a TRO Temporary Restraining Order Against Defendants. Plaintiff seeks $99,000,000,000.00 Billion dollars, a Public warning system if Defendant's are seen on television, and Defendant's to register as sex offenders. Plaintiff prays for relief

1

I've suffered everlasting scarring watching the details on T.V. of each Defendant's acts over the years. It's engrained in my mind. Defendant's must be held accountable for their actions. Think about it... when someone says the name "Michael Jackson", music is not the only thing in my head, I also think child molester. This is Defendant Jackson's fault for doing irreversible damage to my mind

2

The Defendant's collectively injured me through television viewing. When watching and seeing their sexual acts towards minors, women, and themselves, it made me very sick. All these Defendants represent our life. I.e. Public Servants, Entertainers, Religion, Athletes, music, history, our neighbors. My mind is trashed forever.

3

I can't watch the news, the airwaves, newspapers, magazines. I'm disappointed in my leaders. I lost respect to my leaders. I have noone to lookup to.

4

Plaintiff is Afraid to vote because Plaintiff's vote may contribute to putting a sexual predator into office and making Plaintiff feel responsible for contributing to the perversion of America.

5

Plaintiff is now Afraid to use Airport Restrooms because Senator Craig might be lurking in the restroom stalls soliciting sex by attempting to play "footsie" w/ unknown male patrons while relieving themselves

6

Plaintiff is now Horrified of going to A Catholic church because the Priests are out of control. Even last night I had a Nightmare. I was forced to sleep with the Pope in a bulletproof glass bedroom. I can't give confession anymore. I don't know who I'm confessing to. Is he focusing on my confession or my looks / my voice.

7

Plaintiff is scared to go to concerts because Artists like R. Kelly might begin Urinating into the crowd while performing "I believe I can fly"

Plaintiff is also Terrified of going to the Neverland ranch to spend the Night because Michael Jackson might remember the Time when he was a Smooth criminal giving little boys and girls thrillers of their lives while Forcing them to look at the Man in the Mirror while he beat it, then say I want to rock with you all night.

8

Plaintiff is Affraid to Attend College or Pro Basketball or Lacrosse games because players like Kobe Bryant and Duke Lacrosse Guys might lure me to their hotels to pass me around for an assist by other players in an attempt to get their balls in the hole.

9

Plaintiff knows this is new world order. Defendants perverting my skull. I'm affraid to have kids, who is going to protect them in school, church, Sam Goody, or visiting the white house? I can't even appeal to the supreme court because of what Clarence Thomas did to Anita Hill. I expect to be murdered like Rasputin.

Larry Craig was Mitt Romney's top supporter. Romney is a Mormon. Warren Jeffs is a Mormon. This is a conspiracy!

PRELIMINARY INJUNCTION TEMPORARY RESTRAINING ORDER
Plaintiff moves to compel this court to order Defendants to report to their nearest law enforcement office. Branded and labeled. GPS tracked. Cameras installed on them and monitor their movements 24 hours a day. Also forbid Defendants to appear on t.v. worldwide.
    Plaintiff prays for relief

respectfully
submitted
                                    Jonathan Lee Riches ©

Jonathan Lee Riches ©
#40948-018
FCI Williamsburg
P.O. Box 340
Salters, SC 29590
(843) 387-9400

DISTRICT OF ARIZONA

☑ FILED ☑ LODGED
☐ RECEIVED ☑ COPY

SEP 2 4 2007

CLERK U S DISTRICT COURT
DISTRICT OF ARIZONA
BY _____ S DEPUTY

Jonathan Lee Riches ©,
Plaintiff

V.

DMX A/K/A EARL SIMMONS,
DEFENDANT

CIVIL NO:
CV07-01824-PHX-JAT (MHB)

CIVIL COMPLAINT

"ANIMAL ABUSE"

TRO TEMPORARY RESTRAING ORDER

Comes Now the Plaintiff, Jonathan Lee Riches ©, in pro-se, Moves this Honorable to issue an order for Defendant named in this suit to respond. Also moves this Honorable court to issue a Restraining order against Defendant forbidding Defendant from contacting Plaintiff. This suit is civil rights violations and crimes committed by Defendant pursuant to: illegal dog fighting, illegal gambling, Terroristic threats, harassment, and stalking. Plaintiff seeks $6,500,000.00 Million dollars in damages to be donated to SPCA, P.E.T.A, and the Humane Society from Defendant. Plaintiff prays for relief.

Plaintiff, Jonathan Lee Riches ©, is a former body guard and private Investigator for Defendant, currently staying in Salters, South Carolina

Defendant, DMX A/K/A EARL SIMMONS, is a rap artist and actor, currently residing in this county

1

Between September 2004 to August 10, 2007, DMX A/K/A EARL SIMMONS hired me as his personal body guard and private investigator. I looked after DMX following and protecting him on a daily basis. I stayed in a guesthouse provided by DMX on his back property in this county

2

During the time working for DMX I witnessed him abuse and torture numerous animals. This happened during numerous days and times around the world.

3

On June 17, 2007 - DMX broke into a local S.P.C.A and took 3 pomeranian dogs. DMX took them home and fed them to his Pitbulls for personal amusement.

4

May 10, 2007 - This was a event called "doggy night fight". DMX invited Matt Leinart, various Navajo indians, and Stevan Segal to a man made octagon dog fighting ring in back of DMX's property. That afternoon I was in a van with DMX driving around Phoenix snatching dogs from sidewalks, so DMX can use them as "tester dogs" against DMX's Pitbulls. I felt horrible by this, but I had to do what DMX said because he would threaten me and my family.

5

April 10, 2007 - I found out DMX is in distant relations to Fitness Guru Richard Simmons. DMX hired Richard Simmons to be a personal trainer for his Pitbulls. The Pitbulls went through a "sweaten to the oldies" workout.

6

On June 16, 2007, DMX stood out on his balcony at midnight and began howling and shooting arsenal weapons in the air. Endangering his neighbors. DMX also eats out of ALPO bowls

7

On October 7, 2006 - I witnessed DMX doing weird things to fish. We were on a fishing trip to Lake Mead. DMX would catch fish then jump up and down on them. DMX would bark like a dog, foam of the mouth. This odd behavior scared me to death

8

November 10, 2006 - At the rim of the Arizona Grand Canyon DMX was high on drugs. Defendant brought his friend rapper Nelly for sight seeing. DMX made a bet to Nelly that if he threw a cat off the Grand Canyon it would live. I tried to intervene. I told DMX he was a sick man. He just smiled at me and began barking. DMX then threw the cat over the rim. Poor Kitty!

9

Feb 21, 2007 - During a trip to Congo central Africa. DMX would shoot gorillas in the jungle and leave them there.

10

I witnessed DMX kill deer and wildlife without a Licence at Yosemite National Park. This occured on two occations. April 17, 2005 and Feb 24, 2006.

11

On Aug 4, 2007 - DMX and I had a major fallout. DMX recieved a cache of weapons from L.A. Crip gangs in exchange for two kilos of cocaine. DMX took two innocent puppy pit bulls from his dog cage and lined them up in his back yard to shoot. I had enough of this animal abuse. I tried to physically take the UZI away from DMX. DMX pointed the weapon at my head. He also told me "Your Fired white boy". Then turned back towards the dogs and fired his weapon. I was mad and irate, but scared at the same time. DMX kept laughing. I saw the devil in his eyes. DMX said to me "pack Your S--T and get out", told me "If you tell anyone I will kill you". I left the property that day and never worked for DMX again

DMX continues to call and harass me on my cell phone using threats and bodily injury towards me. I changed my cell # three times since Aug 4th, 2007. DMX somehow gets the new number. DMX has alot of connections and I fear for my life.

TRO TEMPORARY RESTRAINING ORDER

For all the reasons previously mentioned, Plaintiff moves this Honorable Court to issue a Restraining order against DMX forbidding DMX from making any harassing phone calls and not to come anywhere near me.

Conclusion

Plaintiff moves this Honorable Court to issue an order for Defendant DMX A/K/A EARL SIMMONS to respond. Plaintiff prays for relief

Respectfully
Submitted

Jonathan Lee Riches ©

Jonathan Lee Riches ©
#40948-018
FCI Williamsburg
P.O. Box 340
Salters, SC 29590
(843) 387-9400

DISTRICT OF NEW JERSEY

Jonathan Lee Riches©,
Plaintiff

V.

COCA-COLA ENTERPRISES INC;
PEPSI COLA BOTTLING GROUP INC;
BRIAR'S USA;
B&E JUICES ENERGY BRANDS;
GLACEAU VITAMIN WATER;
50 CENT A/K/A CURTIS JACKSON;
CANADA DRY BOTTLING CO,
DEFENDANTS

RECEIVED OCT 15 2007
AT 8:30 WILLIAM T. WALSH CLERK

CIVIL NO. 07-4952 (Peny)

RECEIVED OCT 15 2007
AT 8:30 WILLIAM T. WALSH CLERK

Complaint
"Copyright Infringement"
"TRO Temporary Restraining Order"

Comes Now the Plaintiff, Jonathan Lee Riches©, in pro-se, Moves this Honorable Court to issue a Order for Defendants named in this suit to respond. This suit is brought under the Lanham act, copyright Infringement Defendants committed with Jonathan Lee Riches© copyrighted material. Plaintiff moves this Honorable Court to impose declaratory injunctive relief against Defendants distributing Jonathan Lee Riches© copyrighted material on their products and Defendants selling Jonathan Lee Riches© material on google.com and Yahoo.com. Plaintiff moves for a TRO temporary restraining order against Defendants using the Jonathan Lee Riches© Trademarked copyrighted name. Plaintiff seeks $100,000,000.00 Million dollars in damages. Plaintiff requests a Jury trial to hear this case. Plaintiff prays for relief.

1

Since Feb 25th, 2003, Defendants are in a vast conspiracy to use my copyrighted Trademarked name Jonathan Lee Riches© on their products and Advertisements without my consent.

2

Plaintiff is a convicted Identity theft computer hacker serving a illegal sentence of 125 months in Federal prison, currently housed at FCI Williamsburg, Salters South Carolina. Plaintiff's 6th and 8th amendment rights are also being violated under Booker and Foo Fan.

3

Plaintiff received National exposure prior to his Feb 25th, 2003 arrest for his modeling and acting career with Mainline Models in King of Prussia Pennsylvania. Defendant Coca-Cola arranged with Mainline Models on Feb 10, 2001 to have Plaintiff model without his shirt in print and Billboard ads in the Philadelphia/Trenton area drinking Coca-Cola. This was a contract that lasted for 2 years and valued at $250,000 dollars a year. After this contract was terminated, Coca Cola continues to use my Image and copyright name on Billboards Nationwide.

4

Since my arrest Feb 25th, 2003, Defendants use my Image and Photo on all their products. Currently if you buy a 6 pack of Pepsi, on the label you will see "Pepsi cola what Jonathan Lee Riches drinks". Pepsi Cola is distributing my Photographs and the Jonathan Lee Riches© name globally without my permission. This has done my reputation damaged because I don't even like Pepsi. I've always gotten sick in the past drinking Pepsi products.

5

Since Feb 25th, 2003 Rapper 50 cent A/K/A Curtis Jackson, Glaceau vitamin water, Briars USA, and B&E Juices have been putting my name on all their Advertisements without my consent. 50 cents wears Jonathan Lee Riches© T-shirts and Ballcaps in his vitamin water commercials. Glaceau promised to pay Mainline Models $2.5 million dollars to use the Jonathan Lee Riches© copyrighted name

6

Since Feb 25th, 2003, Defendants have used slander and defamation towards my name. Defendants placed a billboard on I-95 10 miles north of South of the Border with my face on it drinking Coca-Cola in one hand, and Pepsi-Cola in the other. It advertised the words "It's so tasty, Even Jonathan Lee Riches drinks it." Jonathan Lee Riches© is now a global brand because of Defendants misconduct without seeking permission from me.

7

On May 10, 2007, I signed a contract with Dreadnaught.wordpress.com. This is the only contract I currently have. Dreadnaught will not write me any letters and I lost contact with them, because they seen me in Defendants advertisements and think I have a contract with them instead. This has caused me major damage.

8

Defendant's plan to host the all you can drink Jonathan Lee Riches© night on my birthday on Dec 27th, 2007 without my consent.

TRO Temporary Restraining Order

I'm suffering bias and prejudice from Defendants conduct, Defendants continue to use my copyright material in Ads, T.V., and the internet. Plaintiffs reputation has been damaged from Defendants conduct, Plaintiff moves this court for a restraining order forbidding Defendants from ever using the Jonathan Lee Riches© name on their products and services. Plaintiff prays for relief.

Respectfully Submitted

Jonathan Lee Riches©
#40948-018
FCI Williamsburg
P.O. Box 340
Salters, SC 29590
(843) 387-9400

Southern District of Texas

Jonathan Lee Riches a/k/a Herb Allison,
Robert Alan Meyst a/k/a Robert Meyst,
Plaintiffs

v.

Hurricane Ike, Hurricane Gustav, Tropical Storm Hannah,
Defendants

United States District Court
Southern District of Texas
FILED
SEP 22 2008
Michael N. Milby, Clerk

I Blame Hurricane IKE for Destroying My Civil Rights
42 USC 1983 / Temporary Restraining Order

Comes now the Plaintiffs Jonathan Lee Riches a/k/a Herb Allison and Robert Alan Meyst a/k/a Robert Meyst, in pro-se, Moves this court to issue an order for Defendants named in this suit to respond. Plaintiffs lives are flooded, we are floating on driftwood. I seek a restraining order against anymore Hurricanes in the Atlantic K-through Z, sea walls build around FCI Williamsburg, a anti Hurricane defense shield built by the army corps of engineers overtop FCI Williamsburg, Plaintiffs face imminent danger from Defendants.

Hurricane Ike blew into the Federal courthouse in Houston and caused significant water damage to Jonathan Lee Riches court records. The Federal courthouse in Houston put Riches's sentencing transcripts on the 1st floor by the front door on purpose to get flooded, warned U.S. Marshal did not protect my court documents, then Hurricane Ike got ahold of the Jonathan Lee Riches Indictment and twisted the facts and linked me with Jeff Skilling and the Enron scandal, Ike caused my brain power to go out on 9-13-08. On the night of 9-12-08 Hurricane Ike blew Houston Astros at our heads from outspace, Houston we have a problem! Because Hurricane IKE NASA launched a secret Govt. spy drone in the air, balistic weather missile test aimed at us at FCI Williamsburg in Salters, S.C., T. Boone Pickens invested in Hurricane Ike's solar wind power. Ike infested me with feline cat 9 lives wind.

Hurricane Ike destroyed my visa and mastercard water paintings. This left me in a tropical depression.
Hurricane Ike caused a spike in my stomach gas, I got cramps. Where is my gas relief in America? Ike stole my laxatives and my levees are holding air tight.

Hurricane Ike is in a secret conspiracy with Barack Obama to destroy G.W. Bush's Texas oil infrastructure to create new Geo-Political U.S. Energy Policies. Ike blew Halliburton to offshore tax havens.

And Hurricane Ike is on OPEC and Wall St. Hedge fund payrolls with Michael Milken, Miss Cleo, betonsports.com, BET Television who put options on gas oil barrel prices to go down under 100 dollars a barrel, while Americans predicted it would go up, using the proceeds to finance more future hurricanes at a secret laboratory in Cern Switzerland.

Hurricane Ike's wind broke apart missing Columbia space shuttle parts in Eastern Texas and blew moon rocks and Houston Rockets into our heads. Johnson Space Center is controlling our minds.
Hurricane Ike broke Yao Ming's foot.
Hurricane Ike blew Bill White, Mayor of Houston's hair off.
Hurricane Ike blew glass from the JP Morgan Chase building into our faces, scarface, a secret revenge for Jonathan Lee Riches sterling Chase visa and mastercards. This is financial terrorism from Defendants. Ike gave us tainted water from Spring Texas.

Hurricane Gustav blew the FCI Williamsburg roofs off.
Hurricane Ike and Whitney Houston took our bodyguards, then Hurricane Ike lifted us up to drown us in Andrea Yates's bathtub.

Ike put our brain on drugs, Any questions?
Hurricane Ike killed our Pepperidge Farm Gold Fish, and Ike swirled in our Dairy Queen Blizzards, Ike tainted Texas land and cattle beef then while the Govt. tricked residents of Galveston for mandatory evacuations they secretly put GPS tracking devices and bugging FISA eavesdropping equipment in residents homes to listen and watch residents Seafood.

The Cuban Govt. formed Hurricane Gustav to allow illegal immigrants to flood into America to attend Mardi Gras and steal U.S. jobs and Castro GTX motor oil.

Tropical Storm Hannah was cousins with Darryl Hannah who splashed onto the shores of South Carolina naked, directly after me because of Riches th tom Hanks castaway look-a-like. See Exhibit (Jonathan Lee Riches unfed and abandoned at FCI Williamsburg). John Candy ate Hurricane Mike n Ikes. Defendants sucked the skin and fat out of my body (see Exhibit). CIA waterboarded tortured me at the beach.

We seek damages. I suffered Thompson water seal damages. Our brains are flooded. Disney Typhoon Lagoon is after us. Defendants illegally changed my copyright name to Johnny Tsunami. Ike beat hurricane Katrina Turner. We sued Hurricane Katrina in Louisiana, Riches v. Hurricane Katrina and Riches v. Fema. Now we are in solitary at FCI Williamsburg in a fish tank, no scuba gear, no lifevests. We face imminent danger from storm surge as all the defendants plan to combine in a mega storm and level our playing field and rip our lives apart, steal our sea shells, assault us with boardwalks and crush our waterfront homes. Defendants are in Good hands with Allstate. We have Exhibits on the next page.
Hurricane Ike was looking for Tina,
Whats Love got to do wit it.

9-14-08

Robert Alan Meyst
Robert Meyst #14871-057
P.O. Box 340
Salters, SC 29590

Jonathan Lee Riches
#40948-018
FCI Williamsburg
P.O. Box 340
Salters, SC 29590
843-387-9400

This is weather warfare. Defendants are planning to destroy Tom Cruise Mission Impossible church of scientology in Clearwater Florida.

Jonathan Lee Riches d/b/a
Gordon Gekko A/K/A
Michael Milken

V.

104th World Series;
Philadelphia Phillies;
Tampa Bay Rays;
Defendants

CASE NO
3:08CV 510

---

42 USC 1983

Preliminary Injunction, Temporary Restraining Order TRO

I face imminent danger from the 2008 World Series, Philadelphia Phillies v. Tampa Bay Rays. The World Series is being shown on the T.V's at FCI Williamsburg. Normally we are locked down at 10pm, cells locked, but because of the defendants, FCI Williamsburg is allowing Late night to watch the world Series until at least 11:45pm, This puts me in danger because my door is unlocked after 10pm, and I could get attacked by Inmate Tampa Bay Rays Fans. I'm from Philadelphia, and my loyalty is to the Phillies, Connie Mack, Mike Schmidt, The Phanatic, Veterans Stadium. The majority of inmates on my unit are from Florida, they hate Philly. I seek a restraining order against the World Series for creating hate, putting my life in danger. Inmates watch Evan Longoria & Pena hit homeruns, and I fear they will use bats at the FCI Williamsburg softball field and swing at my head with them. Aggravated Assault, I'm scared of bodily harm. The 104th World Series must be blacked out from Prison T.V. I pray for relief.

Jonathan Lee Riches d/b/a
Gordon Gekko a/k/a Michael Milken
#40948-018
FCI Williamsburg
P.O. Box 340   843-387-9400
Salters, SC 29590

10-24-08

Jonathan Lee Riches ©,
Plaintiff

Civil No: CV08-2368-PHX-JAT MHB

Matt Leinart; Edgerrin James; Kurt Warner; Larry Fitzgerald; Anquan Boldin; Bertrand Berry; Al Johnson; Gerald Hayes; Chike Okeafor; Reggie Wells; Darnell Dockett; Terrence Holt; Levi Brown; Roderick Hood; Adrian Wilson; Mike Gandy; Antrel Rolle; Alan Branch; Marcel Shipp; Oliver Ross; Aaron Francisco; Sean Morey; Monty Beisel; Terrelle Smith; Chris Cooper; Karlos Dansby; Calvin Pace; Neil Rackers; Brad Badger; Bryant Johnson; Ralph Brown; Nathan Hodel; Ross Kolodziej; Joe Tafoya; Matt Ware; Antonio Smith; Tim Euhus; Oliver Celestin; Tim Rattay; Darryl Blackstock; Elton Brown; J.J. Arrington; Eric Green; Rodney Bailey; Jerheme Urban; Steve Breaston; Keydrick Vincent; Deuce Lutui; Leonard Pope; Gabe Watson; Brandon Johnson; Lyle Sendlein; Troy Bienemann; Tim Castille; Mike Barr; Quentin Moses; Ahmad Merritt; Arizona Cardinals,
Defendants

Temporary Restraining order complaint - I face imminent danger. Plaintiff Jonathan Lee Riches ©, in pro-se, moves under 42 USC 1983 and TRO Temporary Restraining Order. Leinart and his friends are after my life. 42 USC 1983. The "USC" in this statute is the college Leinart went to. I'm in solitary confinement at FCI Williamsburg, this is unconstitutional. Defendants have Victor Conte's Balco phone # in their Apple I-phones and weight trains with Mark Maguire. I compel defendants to take drug testing before each 2008 football game, I believe they are cheating fans. I'm offended by Cardinals ticket pricing. Defendants avoid federal taxes. Defendants run red lights, some of them park in handicap spots illegally. Defendants commit assault on the football team, but local prosecutors are bias to charge them because they watch the assault too. Solitary is keeping me in a cell 24 hours a day, this is a civil rights violation, I seek $25 million. Warner plans to assault me at the Pro Bowl.

Jonathan Lee Riches ©
#40948-018
FCI Williamsburg   843-387-9400
P.O. Box 340
Salters, S.C. 29590

Respectfully Submitted
12-22-08

Jonathan Lee Riches d/b/a MATTHEW J. DYKMAN
Rockefeller Riches, CLERK
Plaintiff CASE NO: 09CV84
MCA/LAM
v.

Lost; Josh Holloway d/b/a James 'Sawyer' Ford; Terry O'Quinn d/b/a John Locke/Jeremy Bentham; Matthew Fox d/b/a Jack Shephard; Evangeline Lilly d/b/a Kate Austin; Naveen Andrews d/b/a Sayid Jarrah; Michael Emerson d/b/a Ben Linus; Elizabeth Mitchell d/b/a Juliet Burke; Jorge Garcia d/b/a Hugo 'Hurley' Reyes; Jeremy Davies d/b/a Daniel Faraday; Rebecca Mader d/b/a Charlotte Lewis; Henry Ian Cusick d/b/a Desmond Hume; Yunjin Kim d/b/a Sun Kwon; Carlton Cuse; Damon Lindelof;
Defendants

Preliminary Injunction, Temporary Restraining Order, TRO
42 USC 1983

Comes Now, Jonathan Lee Riches d/b/a Rockefeller Riches Moves this honorable court for a Preliminary Injunction, Temporary Restraining order Against the ABC Network and their upcoming broadcast of season 5 of Lost. I face imminent danger if this show and defendants are aired on T.V. For the last 5 years every season of Lost has been sending me subliminal messaging and corrupting my mind deeper and deeper into the Abysis. The show ruined my health and mental state. The show Lost and the Defendants destroyed my IQ and caused me a nervous mental reck, I seek full medicare and medicaid benefits when I get released from prison. I seek $200,000,000.00 million dollars in damages, wired to a offshore Cayman Island account. Right now I'm in solitary confinement 24 hour lockdown at FCI Williamsburg because I'm scared to face people because I'm traumatized from watching Lost on the prison TVs. "In solitude, you have no clue, what I'm goin through, alone in this cold room". This is unconstitutional. Defendants gave me inflammation in my colon and now my breath smells like petroleum. Doctors neglect me, and only examine me with electronic impulses on defendants orders. I'm the Lone Ranger in solitary. Defendants took my horse and forced it to race, Smarty Jones. I'm incurable. Lost forced me to lose 45 pounds in 2 weeks, nutrisystem failure. I have mysterious ancient diseases, knee pains. Defendants sold my knee ligaments to Tiger Woods. I got wrinkles in my eyes, throat burn with deep throat whistle blowing against the defendants and crying for help. Jorge Garcia kidnapped me at Bellvue Mental hospital, stole my belly fat and then Sawyer made me jump from a medivac helicopter and handcuffed to the wing of US Airways flight 1549, where I got pneumococcal meningitis and terminal island freeze and a std from Josh Holloway. Josh Holloway kidnapped his sister Natalie Holloway in Aruba and sent her to the Lost Island for covert prostitution. Lost forced me into a romantic 4some with Jack, Kate, Sawyer, Juliet and a bottle of Thousand Island dressing. I was promised by defendants, if I stay in Gilligans Island I get a free continental breakfast. Defendants took me off my meds, drugged me with toxic waste, my membranes has ocean bacteria. I'm a nervous crisis. Defendants conspired with Somali pirates to blow up a freighter, sirius sat. radio. Ben plans to assassinate me then bury me in a LA funeral home with Mr. Bentham. Defendants gave me multiple personalities with Toni Collette. The oceanic 6 CIA water tortured me, gave me Parkinsons disease and a bloody stool. Defendants poisoned me with a

Anesthesiologist, infecting my immune system with 24/7 starvation. Defendants are going to kidnap me at FCI Williamsburg all filmed live on ABC with 13.3 million viewers and time travel me to the Island to make me a survivor contestant in Balls and Chains. I will have to soccer juggle Tom Hanks Wilsons ball and find underground weapons caches with Revenge of the Nerds, and the only way to get off the Island is to spin the Frozen Donkey Wheel. I face danger, harm, and death from defendants. ABC's Lost ~~sugaring of pervasive bad language, sexual explicit material, dirty code~~ language, drug content, and endangering the welfare of federal prison inmates. Because of this show, I'm scared to turn my tv set on. I'm in fear defendants are using their acting salary to contract the poltergeist after me. I move this court to help me. Defendants took my meds and killed Keith Ledger and Jett Travolta and Anna Nicole Smith with my pills. I pray this court will grant my motions and defendants pay me 200 million for relief. I can't watch Barack Obama on the 20th on TV because I'm scared.

respectfully,

1-19-09

Jonathan Lee Riches
d/b/a Rockefeller Riches
FCI Williamsburg
P.O. Box 340
Salters, SC 29590
843-387-9400

Jonathan Lee Riches a/k/a
Johannes Mehserle,
Plaintiff

v.   CV 09-202-PHX-JAT-MHB

Jamal Woolard d/b/a Notorious BIG a/k/a Christopher Wallace; Faith Evans; Susan Sarandon; Josh Brolin; Kara DioGuardi; Neil Patrick Harris; Milla Jovovich; Nick Cannon; Amy Poehler; Meryl Streep; Dev Patel; Viola Davis; Fred Armisen; Kim Raver; Elliot Yamin; D.C. Pierson; Patton Oswalt; Sam Rockwell; Charlyne Yi; Julianne Nicholson; Paul Giamatti; Richard Gere; Ethan Hawke; David Strathaim; Carey Mulligan; Beau Bridges; Patrick McGoohan; Irene Bedard; Fres Oquendo; Radha Mitchell; Tobin Bell; Vin Diesel; Amber Tamblyn; Diane Keaton; Keir O'Donnell; Emma Roberts; Jake T. Austin; Robert Schimmel; Wanda Sykes; Glasvegas; Emeril Lagasse; Diablo Cody; Toni Collette; Anthony "Treach" Criss; Cleavon Little; Gene Wilder; Tom Selleck; Laura San Giacomo; Joshua Close; Clive Owen; Christy Carlson Romano; Dick Van Dyke; Viggo Mortensen; Edward Zwick; Liev Schreiber; Daniel Craig; Peter Fonda; Nick Stahl; Rupert Grint; Frankie Muniz; Bridget Moynahan; Ellen Page; Andre Berto; Hayden Christensen; Teri Garr; Dionne Warwick; Connie Britton; Harley Jane Kozak; Howard Keel; Mira Sorvino; Selena Gomez; Mark Ruffalo; Greg Proops; Alyson Michalka; Kyle Chandler; Amos Lee; Morris Chestnut; Laura Dern; Steve Guttenberg; Gabrielle Union; Delroy Lindo; Nicole de Boer; Patrick Swayze; Leonid Brezhnev; Mary Schapiro; Sophia Loren; Lily Tomlin; Steve Wozniak;

Taraji P. Henson; Gus Van Sant; Mercedes Ruehl; Joe Piscopo; Remo Saraceni; Lauren Ambrose; Mira Sorvino; Rachael Leigh Cook; Adam Lamberg; Phil Spector; Frances McDormand; Colin Firth; Michelle Monaghan; Byron Keith Minns; Piper Perabo; Clementine Eleby; Brad Silberling; Donna Brazile; Eric McCormack; Rosemarie Dewitt; Whitney Port; Claire Forlani; Samantha Mathis; Leah Pipes; Kevin Bacon; Anne Hathaway; Briana Evigan; Jacob Zuma; Kristen Haglund; Ismail Haniya; Richard Umbdenstock; Guy Pierce; Kirsten Gillibrand; Sandy Treadwell; Walt Whitman; Tea Leoni; Zbigniew Brzezinski; Rachel Weisz; Taye Diggs; Ian McShane; Kevin Zegers; Rufus Wainwright; V. Gene Robinson; Barry Pepper; David Alan Grier; Constance Smootz Hevener; Heartland Payment Systems; Oscar de la Renta; Isabel Toledo; Haiyang Zhu; Cyrus Vance; Harold Korell; Camila Alves; Shenae Grimes; Kellan Lutz; Mert Alas; Elena Eustache; Eric Cubiche; Kelly Rutherford; Lauren Conrad; Sara Jean Underwood; Kate Bosworth; Maria Menounos; Elisha Cuthbert; Goumba Johnny; Emily Vancamp; Ali Larter; Amanda Seyfried; Deryck Whibley; Daphne Brogden; Ritmo Mundo; Audrina Patridge; Katherine Heigl; January Jones; Aimee Teegarden; Leighton Meester; Spencer Pratt; Brian Austin Green; Tricia Helfer; Gabrielle Anwar; Billie Piper; Gordon Ramsay; Jasmine Dimilo; Malin Akerman; Hoda Kotb; Colbie Caillat; Jeremy Camp; Michael Manning Weatherly Sr; Vanessa Marcil; Tyrese Gibson; Stacy Keibler; Kate Winslet; Ted Marchibroda; Stacy Ann Ferguson; Norm Duke; Kirsten Dunst; Glenn Close; Bon Iver; Cicely Tyson;

Jane Monheit; Dwayne De Rosario; Naomi Campbell; Gaby Gibson; Kevin Durant; Brandon Roy; Amare Stoudemire; Andrew Bogut; Chauncey Billups; Marcus Camby; Russ Grimm; Shanna Moakler; Rebecca Mader; Rachel Zoe; Dominic Purcell; Naomi Foner; Rajon Rondo; Elton Brand; Claude Lemieux; Dwyane Wade; Naomi Watts; Agyness Deyn; Jared Kushner; Cacee Cobb; Derrick Favors; Andris Biedrns; Yao Ming; Paz Vega; Herschel Walker; Andrew Dice Clay; Eden Gaha; Dennis Rodman; Jennie Garth; Jason Priestley; Craig Kilburn; Jimmy Fallon; Ricardo Montalban; Craig Ferguson; Ellen Burstyn; Leslie Sansone; Jesse Metcalfe; Bonnie Huntshow; Charles Mattocks; Zach Braff; Howie Mandel; Amber Lee Ettinger; Kyle Born Keller; Tavis Smiley; Crooked X; Laura Linney; Jett Travolta; Regis Philbin; Dustin Hoffman; Benjamin R. Barber; Fred Armisen; Brooke Nevin; Herbie Slavin; Barry Minkow; Shane Mosley; Anna Torv; Luke Janklow; Howie Dorough; Stedman Graham; Jennifer Love Hewitt; Alonzo Mourning; Randolph L. Cook; George O'Dowd; Dina Ruiz; Terry Semel; Drew Gilpin Faust; Windell Middlebrooks; Parminder Nagra; Percy Harvin; Vladimir Kagan; Maya Moore; Rex Ryan; Pete Maravich; Ken Whisenhunt; Prince Fielder; Kevin Garnett; Paul Pierce; Ray Allen; Moses Malone; Vince Carter; Charles Barkley; Jane Lubcheno; Shane Dronett; Curt Schilling; DeBanhams; Ted Leonis; Ali Al-Marri; Nicole Fawcett; David Duval; Peja Stojakovic; Tyson Chandler; Tracy McGrady; Dwight Howard; Hedo Turkoglu; Romain Dumas; Charlie Villanueva; Johnny Weir; Susie Essman; Michelle Kwan; Kay Yow; Gretchen Bleiler; Bertrand Delanoe; Molly Shannon; Memo Rojas; AJ Allmendinger; Neil Gaiman; Claudette Mink; Max Papis;

Miles Brand; Kathleen Quinlan; Monica Bellucci; Hugh Laurie; Gabrielle Union; Cole Hamels; Larry Fitzgerald; Troy Polamalu; Antwaan Randle El; Seve Ballesteros; Fred Armisen; Mexx; Eugene Levy; Deborah Raffin; Rhona Mitra; Nadia Bjorlin; Arthur Nadel; Xi Jinping; Joshua Durcho; Alan Cumming; Bill Bidwell; Moammar Gadhafi; Dan Rooney; Alonso Compean; Ignacio Ramos; Osvaldo Aldrete Davila; Raffaello Follieri; Sebastian Hizey; R. Donahue Peebles; Moctar Ould Jiddou; ~~[redacted]~~ PBS Nightly Business Report; Hollywood.com; Cliff Anicelli; Paul Dergarabedian; Verne Troyer; Campbell Mithun; Nicklas Lidstrom; Pavel Datsyuk; Dante Lavelli; Peanut Corporation of America; Golden Raspberry Awards; Emeka Okafor; Chris Paul; Kimmie Meissner; Troy Aikman; Chris Collinsworth; Chris Myers; Ron Jaworski; Tony Kornheiser; John Madden; Phil Simms; Joe Buck; Jim Nantz; Bob Costas; Al Michaels; Jim Nantz; Bob Papa; Mike Tirico; Chris Berman; Rich Eisen; Curt Menefee; Peter King; James Brown; Charley Casserley; Jay Glazer; Chris Mortensen; Adam Schefter; Tony Siragusa; Pam Oliver; Andrea Kremer; Howie Long; Keyshawn Johnson; Dan Marino; Brian Billick; Dan Marino; Bill Cowher; Steve Mariucci; Jeremy Schaap, Defendants

Preliminary Injunction, Temporary Restraining order, TRO 42 USC 1983

Comes now, Jonathan Lee Riches a/k/a Johannes Mehserle, I face imminent danger and bodily harm from all the defendants listed. I seek a restraining order. I face imminent death and torture from Defendants. All the listed Defendants are conspiring and financially

DISTRICT OF DELAWARE

-09- 077

Jonathan Lee Riches a/k/a
Joshua David Duhamel,
Plaintiff

v.

The National Enquirer d/b/a American Media Inc;
Star Magazine; Reginald Fitz; Don Gentile; Michael
Glynn; Rick Egusquiza; Alan Butterfield; Lynn Allison;
John Blosser; Lynette Holloway; John Combs; Michael
Cherico; Lisa Luchesi; Patricia Shipp; Len Feldman; Larry
Haley; Philip Smith; Sharon Ward; Annette Witheridge;
David Gardner; Jeff Samuels; David Wright; Laurie Miller;
Alan Smith; Deborah Hughes; Mike Walker; Susan Baker;
Dorothy Cascerceri; Alexander Hitchen; Matt Coppa;
Candace Trunzo; Heidi Parker; Sandra Clark; Matthew
Mundy; Alex Burton; Jennifer Pearson; Casey Brennan;
Melissa Cronin; Tim Plant; Kathleen Perricone; Kate
Major; Mike Olson; Jennifer Angel,
Defendants

Preliminary Injunction, Temporary Restraining order, TRO
42 USC 1983

Comes now, Jonathan Lee Riches a/k/a Joshua David Duhamel, Moves this Honorable Court for a TRO, Temporary Restraining order, TRO & a Preliminary Injunction Against The National Enquirer Magazine, Star magazine which are both owned by American Media Inc and a List of Defendants who are reporters and Editors for these Magazines. I face imminent danger and Bodily harm from all the Defendants who are threatening to publish my story, including me being in Federal prison for stealing multiple celebrities identities, credit & credit cards in their names which got me 125 months in Federal prison, and they plan to publish court records of mine of me suing thousands of celebrities nationwide for violating my civil rights. From July 10, 2008 through December 30, 2008, I have recieved over 450 letters and Phone calls by Defendants at FCI Williamsburg in Salters S.C. which the Defendants are requesting interviews and my side of the story, and Defendants said on Each letter if I don't cooperate with them, they will write horrible negative articles about me to embarass my character, and they said they will not stop calling here. FCI Williamsburg and the warden were sick of the Defendants calling here everyday asking to speak or interview me, that they Locked me up in Solitary confinement, 24 hour a day Lockdown for security reasons. This is where I'm writing this suit, without a typewriter. This is torture. Defendants are responsible for me suffering and possibly dying in solitary confinem. I'm Freezing cold, I have no windows, I get fed through a slot in the door like a dog, rats on my floor, Anti-white Graffati on the walls, I'm subjected to used oversized clothing. I'm starving I weigh only 119 lbs at 5 ft 10 inches, my ribs stick out. FCI Williamsbu is shipping me on Diesel therapy and Punishing me because of the Defendants conduct and Defendants relentless harassment on me and to this facility to interview me. Defendants sent reporters to the front gates of FCI Williamsburg camped out trying to speak with me. Defendants tried to call here posing as my sick mother. Defendants also called here saying my Father died in a car accident, so the chaplain would get me on the Phone. Defendants are trying to bribe me with mone or a free subscription to their magazines. Now FCI Williamsburg and the warden says they will not let me out of solitary confinement and told me to "Rot in Hell" as long as Defendants keep calling and sending letters to the prison harassing me for a interview. I'm going to die in here, I have no access to a phone or my personal property. Defendants have baby pictures and mug shot pictures they illegally obtained from the Bureau of prisons of me. Also, CNN presents "How to Rob a Bank" did a feature story on me in which CNN provided the National Enquirer with audio tapes and evidence of me doing identity theft and fraud in celebrities names. I was accused of stealing Sean P. Diddy Combs citibank card with 15 thousand and adding a authorized user in the name of Christy Combs in 2002. I took identities from Janet Reno, Bob Barker, Sean Penn, Lindsay Lohan, Chris Rock, and many more. I'm paying for my crimes and just want to be left alone by defendants. Please stop stalking me National Enquirer's they created Havoc on my Life. I have nightmares I'm scared they are going to endanger my privacy and put feature articles on me in their magazines and websites. I seek a restraining order preventing defendants from publishing, printing or posting photos with me or anything affiliate with my life. I also seek 10 million dollars in damages, emotional distress and trauma. I pray this court will grant my motions for relief.

respectfully,

Jonathan Lee Riches a/k/a
Joshua David Duhamel
#40948-018
FCI Williamsburg   843-387-9400
P.O. Box 340
Salters, SC 29590

1-25-09

Jonathan Lee Riches d/b/a
Bernard Madoff,
Plaintiff

CASE NO: 4:09CV252-DCB

V.

I can't Believe it's Not Butter; Piggly Wiggly 2% milk; Kraft Miracle Whip; Tums Ultra; StarKist Chunk Light Tuna; Oscar Mayer Bacon; Pasta Roni; Kroger Savory Rotisserie chicken; Kellogg's Frosted Flakes; Pepperidge Farm GoldFish Crackers; Kool-Aid Jammers; Ho Ho Ho Green Giant Beans; U.S.D.A Select Black Canyon Angus Beef; Little DeBBie oatmeal Cream Pies; Van Camp's Baked Beans; Pillsbury Biscuits; Angel Soft Bath Tissue; Cascade Dish Detergent; Juicy Juice; Deer Park Natural spring water; Gatorade thirst Quencher; Tombstone original Pizza; Kid Cuisine meals; FeBreze FaBric Refresher; Puffs Facial Tissue; Neosporin First Aid; Mennen Speed stick; Ensure Nutrition Shakes; Yoplait Go-Gurt Portable Yogurt; Coffee-mate coffee creamer; Dawn Dish Liquid; Chef Boyardee Mini Ravioli; Minute Rice; Red Gold Tomato Ketchup; Ragú Pasta sauce; Peter Pan Peanut Butter; Hunt's Manwich Sloppy Joe sauce; Duke's mayonnaise; Betty Crocker suddenly salad mix; Sweet Sue Chicken & Dumplings; NaBisco 100 Calorie Packs; Tennessee Pride Pork sausage; Washington Extra Fancy FuJi Apples; El Monterey Mexican Appetizers; Mrs. Weaver's Pimento cheese spread; Pilgrim's Pride chicken thighs; Wampler's Meat Corn Dogs; Fischer's sliced Bologna; Food Lion Apple Juice; Edy's Butter Pecan; Scott Bath Tissue; DiGiorno Pizza; Butcher's Brand T-Bone Steak; Hamburger Helper; A1 Steak Sauce; Gillette Fusion; Packham Pears; Hillshire Farm select ultra thin lunch meats; Jamestown Brand Roll sausage; Food Lion Meatballs; T.G.I. Friday's Frozen Appetizers; Freschetta Pizza; Coppertone Sun care;

Klondike Ice Cream Bars; Ore-Ida Potatoes; Weight Watchers Smart Ones Dinners; Edge Shaving Gel; Purina Dog Chow; Pam Cooking Spray; Wisk Liquid Detergent; Lipton Tea; Zesta Crackers; Doritos; Ruffles; Tostitos; Wesson Oil; Oreo Cookies; Heinz Vinegar; Russell Stover Boxed Chocolate; Rice Krispies Treats; Motts Apple Sauce; Country Time Lemonade; Planters Trail Mix; Sour Patch Kids; Swedish Fish; Twizzlers; Tootsie Roll Pops; Skittles; Starburst; Dum Dums; Orville Redenbacher Popcorn; Hershey's Kisses; 3 Musketeers; 100 Grand; ~~Nestle Butterfinger~~; Reese's Peanut Butter Cups; ~~Maxwell House Coffee~~; Pampers; Depend Underwear for Men or Women; Always Maxi Pads; Tampax Tampons; Hawaiian Tropic Suncare; GE Reveal Light Bulbs; Oral B Toothbrush; Jelly Beans; Effergrip; Animal Crackers; Spam; Mrs. Dash Extra Spicy; Twix; Pico Pica Hot Sauce; Wheatables; Ramen Roast Chicken Soup; Mountain Dew; Noxzema; St. Ives Apricot Scrub; Petroleum Jelly; Sudafed 24 hour; Triple Antibiotic Ointment; Bengay; Hydroxycut; Zantrex; Soy Joy; Lamisil; Durex Condoms; K-Y Intense Arousal Gel; Just For Men; ConAir Electric Razors; Norelco; Old Spice; Ginseng; Leptopril; Promensil; Twinlab Supplements; Hollywood 48 hour miracle diet; Osteo Bi-Flex; Downy Softener; Country of Hungary; Dole Foods; Baskin-Robbins; Pilgrim's Pride Corp; Carvel Corp; Keebler Co.; Barq's Root Beer; American Crystal Sugar Co; Sara Lee Bakery; McCormick & Co; Mrs. Smith's Frozen Foods Co; Alpo Pet Foods; Domino Sugar Corp; Frito-Lay; Entenmann's; Ocean Spray Cranberries; Hormel Foods Corp; The Quaker Oats Corp; Schepps Dairy; Jim Beam Brands Co.; Bacardi Imports; Shasta Beverages; Welch Grape Juice; Hanover Foods; Trinidad-Benham Corp; Conagra; Metz Baking; Omaha Steaks International; Eagle Snacks; Sysco Corp; Coors Brewing Co; Tillamook County Creamery Assn; Amcor Capital Corp.; Captain Crunch Cereal; Tom's Foods; The Spice Girls; Juan Valdez; Food Poisoning Inc; The U.S. Food Pyramid, Defendants

Preliminary Injunction, Temporary Restraining Order, TRO
I face Imminent Danger & Bodily Harm from these Food Products

Complaint

Comes Now, Jonathan Lee Riches d/b/a Benard Madoff, I face imminent danger from all the defendants foods that the Bureau of Prisons have been forcing into my body since the very first day I was illegally incarcerated on Feb 25th 2003, which violates my 8th amendment rights for cruel and unusual punishment. I'm currently at Federal Medical Center Lexington Kentucky where they continue to serve me the defendants, which is rotten, uncooked food laced with poisonous chemicals and toxins that are destroying my body. I can't believe it's not butter, clogs my arteries, and raised my blood pressure so high that I've suffered different strokes. Defendants cause me daily heartburn and indigestion that are ripping my insides apart. After drinking Piggly Wiggly 2% milk and oreo cookies every night at 9pm before I go to bed, I get diahreah and throw up in the toilet, this is a deliberate plot by the defendants to shut my kidneys & liver down. Defendant's cause me Irritable Bowel syndrome. Defendant's gave me E coli and other mysterious illnesses which caused me to lose to much weight. I weigh only 107 lbs at 5ft 10 inches. I'm becoming a walking skeleton because the defendants endangers my body and enter my nervous system daily. Defendants nutrients, herbs n spices are ripping my insides to pieces. Defendants caused me to get a colon exam. I'm so weak and anemic from defendants that I can't type this lawsuit. I seek better nutrition and a doctor to examine me before I die from defendants. Federal prison is genocide and a Holocaust with foods that are torturing me. Defendants are cursing my mental instability. Defendants products must be taken off the shelves for relief. I seek a Injunction against these foods being put in my body, these defendants food labels lie, I'm receiving way more fiber in defendants products then advertised which is causing me to use the toilet #2 30 times a day. I seek FDA intervention, I seek a full investigation of these products. I'm dying. Please help me before the defendants murder my life. Dia Sawents I pray for relief.

Jonathan Lee Riches #40948018
Federal Medical Center
P.O. Box 14500
Lexington, KY 40512
859-255-6812

Respectfully,
4-27-09

Bernard Madoff d/b/a
Jonathan Lee Riches a/k/a
Jonathan L. Riches Investment Securities LLC,
Plaintiff

V.

Bank of America corp; Merrill Lynch & co; Kenneth Lewis; Danny Pang d/b/a Private Equity Management Group Inc a/k/a PemGroup; California Public Employees' Retirement System, Calpers,
Defendants

FILED
UNITED STATES DISTRICT COURT
ALBUQUERQUE, NEW MEXICO

MAY 4 – 2009

MATTHEW J. DYKMAN
CLERK

CIV-09-486 JB RHS

Preliminary Injunction, Temporary Restraining Order, TRO

I face imminent danger and bodily harm from Defendants. Bank of America is withholding Americans Ponzi money and used my 50 Billion dollars to invest in subprime loans. Danny Pang aided and abetted in my identity theft and his Pemgroup is a secret offshore bank account holding fraud money. Calpers stole my social security # opened Bernard Madoff dollar store Accounts and Piggly Wiggly Supermarket accounts. Kenneth Lewis threatend to merge Riches and Madoff in a Investment marriage in San Francisco. Bank of America financed my wire frauds, Merrill Lynch & co is threatening to hang me for looting Tyco. I'm so scared of defendants, I would not leave my penthouse for weeks. Bank of America gave me loans to bet on Mets games, to buy Mets season tickets and I got swine Flu in a New Mexico Bank of America Branch. Kenneth Lewis illegally used my Ponzi money to pay ransoms to Somali Pirates. Defendants cooperated with the Patriot Act and gave Madoff & Riches files to the Government illegally. Defendants caused me emotional distress and I will never use defendants banks again. Kenneth Lewis is a corporate raider he is trying to oust members of the Jonathan L Riches Investment Securities Board and Replace it with Emmanuel Lewis (webster), Carl Lewis, Lewis & Clark, Lewis Skolnick (lamda lamda lamda), Leona Lewis. Reggie Lewis gave me a heart attack. I seek a restraining order against defendants

Jonathan Lee Riches #40448018
Federal Medical Center
P.O. Box 14500
Lexington, KY 40512
859-255-6812

respectfully,
[signature] 5-1-09

Jonathan Lee Riches d/b/a 3:09-cv-00267
Bernard Madoff a/k/a
Bernard L. Madoff,
Plaintiff

V.

MoonLite Bunny Ranch; Jenna Jameson; Sex.com a/k/a www.sex.com; Adam & Eve; PlayBoy Magazine; Mustang Ranch; Peter North; Ron Jeremy; Madame Tussaud's Wax Museum; American Curves Magazine; Dennis Hof; Heidi Fleiss; Brothel in Pimlico; Adult Entertainment; Stuff Magazine; Escourt.com; Vivid Entertainment; craigslist.com; whorehouse;
Defendants

---

28 USC 1331
Preliminary Injunction, Temporary Restraining Order, TRO

Comes Now, Jonathan Lee Riches d/b/a Bernard Madoff a/k/a Bernard L. Madoff, I face imminent danger and Bodily harm. This court has Jurisdiction as the MoonLite Bunny Ranch is in the Reno Nevada Area, its owner Dennis Hof, and the List of the Defendants who occupy and stay there with illegal operations of Prostitution over Interstate lines and the Defendants have been harassing me relentlessly with vaction travel packages to the MoonLite when I get out of prison. Defendants send me underage pornography in the mail. Defendant Jenna Jameson told me in a Feb 14th, 2009 valentines letter that if I payed her $5000 and add her to my prison visiting List at Federal Medical Center in Lexington Kentucky she would perform sexual acts on me under the table in the visiting room. I don't know how Jameson got my address but I take offense to the prostitution offer as I'm a born again Christian in prison, so help me Jesus. Then Jameson & Ron Jeremy want to perform porno movies with me for Vivid Entertainment because of my Internet celebrity status and me formally working as a Editor for Playboy Magazine. Someone added Jonathan Lee Riches to the Sex Advertisement Section on craigslist.com and since then Heidi Fleiss & Peter North have been sexually harassing me and want me to start a Escourt business with them at a male stud Ranch in Reno to accept credit cards then have me steal the studs & customers credit cards to ⟨...⟩ Naughty Langere and sex toys from Adam & Eve Free, American Curves Plans to put me in their July 2009 center fold naked, this is a invasion of privacy. Whore houses and Brothels nationwide are in a secret conspiracy with female inmates in federal prisons to be Escorts and Prostitutes for the Defendants as part of a plea bargin deal, in return females get early parole and unlimited TB testing. The Defendants sexual conduct is a act of Satan. Jenna Jameson corrupted Nuns to work at the Moonlite covertly, the Moonlite hosted the D.C. Madam who brought Sen. Harry Reid and Arlen Specter to the Moonlite Bunny Ranch for rest and relaxation with Democratic escorts, political Prostitutes. Madame Tussaud's wax museum is waxing a sculpture of me, the Jonathan Lee Riches Exhibit, with a crown, credit card czar, the Defendants outsource prostitutes to Iranian mullahs, a violation of the trading with the Enemy Act. Also, I witnessed Barack Obama entering the Moonlite on 10 occasions buying Escorts with campaign money and Michelle Obama used the Stimulus Package funds to get back rubs by Peter North. The whores at the Moonlite turned me into a pervert, I can't hold a normal relationship with a catholic Priest. Defendants endangered my health, gave me sexually transmitted diseases, Now I weigh 110 lbs and can't get it up, I can't produce kids because Defendants ruined me, Defendants stole my Cialis bathtub, Adam & Eve sexually Assaulted me in the garden of Eden, Everytime I see a women, I hide in the closet. Defendants stole my Blowup dolls, My _enis Pumps. The Defendants are corrupting the world, I have a Judicial duty to stop this evilness as our Youth are in danger and Defendants teach rapists to rape, child molesters congregate at the Moonlite, I saw John Mark Karr there in 2000 with Jon Benet Ramsey in Room 8. I seek the destruction of the Moonlite, Defendants forced into sex therapy, Injunctions and restraining orders against Defendants sexually insulting and corrupting my mind and ruining my sex drive. I want to have kids one day, Defendants Broke into my sperm Bank, this is a Ponzi scam. I seek relief.

respectfully,

Jonathan Lee Riches d/b/a Bernard Madoff
#40948018 Federal Medical Center
P.O. Box 14500
Lexington, KY 40512   859-255-6812

9-18-09

Jonathan Lee Riches d/b/a
Omar AL-Bashir a/k/a
Robert Mugabe,   CASE NO: 4:09-cv-298-DCB
Plaintiff

V.

Jiverly A. Wong; American Civic Association; Gander Mountain; Parveen Ali; Almir O. Alves; Marc Henry Bernard; Maria Sonia Bernard; Hai Hong Zhong; Lan Ho; Jiang Ling; Hong Xiu Mao; Layla Khalil; Roberta "Bobby" King; Li Guo; Dolores Yigal; Maria Zobniw; James Harrison; Richard Poplawski; Shirley DeLucia,
Defendants

Preliminary Injunction, Temporary Restraining Order, TRO

Comes now, Jonathan Lee Riches d/b/a Omar Al-Bashir a/k/a Robert Mugabe. I face imminent danger from the defendants who are planning to massacre me on Easter Holiday to steal my financial nest eggs. Jiverly A. Wong stole handguns from the D.C. Heller case and he plans to shoot my eye out with a Red Rider BB gun. Wong is mad at me because I was a former 4 star general from the Vietnam War. Defendant Wong said that me and Charlie Sheen killed his family in Platoon and Wong said I conspired with Robin Williams to wake him and his wife up each morning on the radio. The American Civic Association stole my used Honda and the rest of the Defendants plan to rise from the Dead, Dawn of the Dead, Thriller, to eat my brains for being a smart aleck. Wong secretly text messaged Cho from Virginia Tech. Wong had posters on his wall of Dillon Klebold and Eric Harris. Wong claims I'm a capitalist who corrupted China and Wong said I put lead in his toys and got his pit bulls sick that Wong bought from Michael Vick in Wongs dog food. Wong tried to burn me on the Chinese New Year 2008 with Wong tong soup. Wong is responsible

For my illegal incarceration, on Feb 25th, 2003 Defendant Wong sent Agent Orange from Houston FBI to detain me in the Hanoi Hilton with John McCain, Wong burned Pol Pot tatoos in my skin and Wong shot a Magnum P.I. handgun in my temple. Wong stole my full metal jacket that I got at Neverland belonging to Mic Jackson with the zippers. Wong assaulted me on a Boy Scout nature hike along the Ho Chi Ming trail in 1986, Me and Michael Jay Fox were a casualty of war because of Wong. Gander mountain is a alias to Brokeback mountain and Wong planned to marry Wen Ho Lee to obtain Binghamton NY nuclear secrets. I'm in fear of Wong, he is still alive as the messiah and Wong said I stole his identity. Wong & the defendants plan to come to the Federal Medical Center in Lexington Kentucky where I'm at and shoot my brains, CIA water torture me and Vietnam con me into a ponzi scam to pay for Bernard Madoffs defense. Wong jined the Vietnam chapter of Al-qada and wants to behead my Jewish head. Wong wrote me death threats by firing squad, Wong tried to hang me Jena 6, Wongs eyes are slanted. I'm in major fear for my life. Wong planted a mine field around me, I'm subjected to white foso furous, Wong is sending Somali pirate ships to hijack my booty in a sexual assault. I seek a restraining order against the defendants. I pray this court will grant my motions for emergency relief.

respectfully,

Jonathan Lee Riches #40948018
Federal Medical Center
P.O. Box 14500
Lexington, KY 40512
859-255-6812

4-9-09
4-9-09

DISTRICT OF ARIZONA

Bernard Madoff d/b/a
Jonathan Lee Riches,
Plaintiff

v.

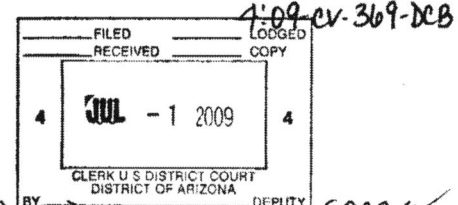

American Curves Magazine d/b/a Americancurvesmag.com; Robert Kennedy; Comag Marketing Group; Jerry Kindela; Rico Marques; Sarah Wells; Dean Brierly; John Eagan; Gino Edwards; Rob March; Cecily Knobler; TJ Thomas; Bev Greene; Kevin Greene; Gill Daniels; Trevor Ratz; The Capris Group; Carolyn Zaum; Judy Cancelliere; Todd Hughes; Holly Burns; Tony Piazza; Alicia Abela; Amanda Scazzariello; Corrado Mallia; Vincent Antonellis; Jeff Maltby; Lisa Snow; Lynda Sammut; Sarah Leslie; Janna Ireland; Kim Moore; Christopher Barnes; Leigh Hargrove; Erin Morris; Paul Buceta; Irvin Gelb; Alex Ardenti; Eric Freimanis; David Paul; Michael Palmer; Ricardo Marconi; Andy McFarland; Todd Plinke; Rob Sims; Terry Goodlad; Scott Appleby; Justin Price,
Defendants

Filed/Received JUL -1 2009
Clerk U S District Court
District of Arizona
4:09-cv-369-DCB

28 USC 1331

Preliminary Injunction, Temporary Restraining Order

I face imminent danger and bodily harm from the Defendants American Curves magazine and all their staff who obtained illegal pictures of my mugshot along with private photos the FBI collected when they raided my Penthouse, and American Curves plans to feature me as a cover boy for their July 2009 magazine and place me in their centerfold. American Curves has pictures of me in Richie Rich trunks next to Dollar my dog surrounded by 100 dollar bills smoking a Cuban in my bathtub, this photo was taken by Farrah Fawcett and American Curves got pictures of me swimming naked in the French Riviera, and American Curves staff keep harassing me in prison trying to get a interview from me and tell my side of the story. Defendants threatened me with body surgery if I don't talk to them. Defendants discriminate against female inmates, they don't feature any prisoners in their magazines, this is a EEOC violation and discrimination. Defendants overcharge their magazine, as I'm poor now making only .12¢ a month sweeping bird droppings on the sidewalk in chains, and picking up guards cigarette butts, which is unconstitutional.

I hold American Curves Magazine liable for my Erectional disfunction, their women do not satisfy me and I'm forced to pay $4.99 to see women who caused me genital warts. Defendant's use female models that are under 18 from the Inner streets of cities. In the May Issue, I saw a picture of my neighbor Lola who is only 13, this is child porn, Defendants are liable. I got Assaulted by a homosexual inmate on 6-16-09 who stole my American Curves Fed. Issue, rolled it up, Beat my head to a pulp. The Defendants models killed David Caridine in thailand. American Curves staff is financed with my Ponzi money, American Curves is distributed to Iranian Youths in Mosques and American Curves Magazines discriminates against female Eskimo's, when did you ever see a Eskimo in their magazine. I opened up and turned the page on the Nov. 2008 American Curves and got a paper cut, American Curves is liable, American Curves double billed my credit card for 999 Issues. American Curves Rattled my American Nerves, the models are fake, they are Airbrushed with prison paint, American Curves are illegally Advertising my legal expertize in their classifieds, I called 1900-Lines Advertised in American Curves and got the wrong horiscope, instead I got threatened by the Zodiac Killer. American Curves their females are really males from hong kong. I'm in serious danger and seek protection. Defendant's are sending U.S. Drone planes to spy on me for the NSA, to photograph me for 60 minutes and sell my face to Anderson Cooper 360, No Spin Zone, Bill O'Reilly, O'Reilly Auto Part Assault me. I seek protection

Bernard Madoff d/b/a 6-27-09
Jonathan Lee Riches
#40948018
Federal Medical Center
P.O. Box 14500
Lexington, KY 40512

Jonathan Lee Riches
Bernard L. Madoff
Bernie Madoff,
Plaintiff

v.

Global Warming; An Inconvenient Truth; Al Gore; Carbon Dioxide; Greenhouse Gases; National Geographic; Tropic of Cancer; Tropic of Capricorn; Ethanol; Ozone Layer; U.S. Clean Air Act; Northern Hemisphere; Oxygen; Isotopes; Methane; Nitrous Oxide; Kristin Gore; Tipper Gore; Karenna Gore Schiff; Drew Schiff; Wyatt Schiff; Frank Hunger; Paul Cusack; Current T.V.; Earth in the Balance; Ecology and the Human Spirit; Generation Investment Management; Atmosphere; Jeff Skoll; Participant Productions; Melcher Media; Joel Hyatt; CO_2 Emissions; Sulfur Hexafluoride; Roger Revelle; Carbonic Acid; Tundra; Greenland; Glaciers; Mount Kilimanjaro; Arctic Sea; Antarctica; World Meteorological Organization; Siberia; Solar Energy; Toyota Hybrid,
Defendants

RECEIVED BY MAIL
MAR 22 2010
U.S. DISTRICT COURT
EASTERN DISTRICT OF MO
ST. LOUIS

[28 USC 2241
HABEAS CORPUS RELIEF
28 USC 1331]

The manner in which my sentence was executed is unconstitutional. I Jonathan Lee Riches d/b/a Bernard L. Madoff faces imminent danger and bodily harm from the defendants. My 8th amendment rights are being violated for cruel and unusual punishment. Defendants are creating a deliberate indifference on my life in St. Louis and globally. Farmer v. Brennan. My 6th amendment rights are being violated under U.S. v. Booker and U.S. v. Fanfan. Global warming has done me so much mental stress and physical hardship over the years. Lets start with my skin. I think I have skin cancer on the scalp on top my head all caused by global warming and the rays of the sun beating down on my head every summer since I been illegally incarcerated

IN THE UNITED STATES DISTRICT COURT
DISTRICT OF ARIZONA

UMAR FAROUK ABDULMUTALLAB;
JONATHAN LEE RICHES;
PLAINTIFF;S

V.

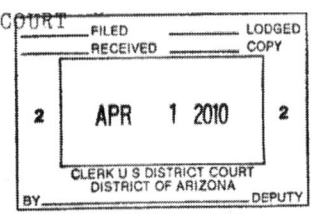

ABC's DANCING WITH THE STARS; NICOLE SCHERZINGER; DEREK
HOUGH; KATE GOSSELIN; TONY DOVOLANI; ERIN ANDREWS; MAKSIM
CHMERKOVSKIY; CHAD OCHOCINCO; CHERYL BURKE; EVAN LYSACEK;
ANNA TREBUNSKAYA; NIECY NASH; LOUIS VAN AMSTEL; BUZZ ALDRIN;
ASHLY COSTA; AIDEN TURNER; EDYTA SLIWINSKA; PAMELA ANDERSON;
DAMIAN WHITEWOOD; SHANNEN DOHERTY; MARK BALLAS; JAKE
PAVELKA; CHELSIE HIGHTOWER,
DEFENDANT'S

CIV10- 191TUCDCB

PRELIMINARY INJUNCTION ~~TEMPORARY RESTRAINING ORDER~~

COMES NOW, THE PLAINTIFFS UMAR FAROUK ABDULMUTALLAB AND
JONATHAN LEE RICHES, WE FACE IMMINENT DANGER AND BODILY HARM
FROM THE DEFENDANTS COLLECTIVELY AND INDIVIDUALLY.
THE DEFENDANTS ARE DISCRIMINATING AGAINST ARE MUSLIM FAITH
BY PROMOTING ADULTRY AND DANCING IS FORBIDDEN IN ISLAM AND
WE ARE BEING FORCED TO WATCH THE DEFENDANTS ENJOY THEMSELVES
ON TELEVISION WHILE BILLIONS OF PEOPLE IN THE WORLD CAN NOT
AFFORD A TV SET, DEFENDATS DONT CARE ABOUT GLOBAL HUNGER AND
DEFENDANTS DIRTY DANCING ACTS OFFENDS US, AND PROMOTES
SEXUAL ACTIVITY FOR MINORS WATCHING THE SHOW, THIS IS A DANGER
TO SOCIETY THAT THE DEFENDATS ARE CONTRIBUTING TO, SO WE SEEK
A RESTRAING ORDER AS OUR MORALS AND VALUES WILL SUFFER IF THE
DEFENDATS CONTINUE THESE CRIMINAL ACTS ON TV. WE PRAY THIS
COURT WILL GRANT OUR MOTION FOR RELIEF.

RESPECTFULLY,

UMAR FAROUK ABDULMUTALLAB 3-28-10
PO BOX 14500
LEXINGTON, KY 40512

JONATHAN LEE RICHES 3-29-10
40948-018
PO BOX 14500
LEXINGTON, KY 40512

IN THE UNITED STATES DISTRICT COURT
FOR THE MIDDLE DISTRICT OF TENNESSEE

FILED
U.S. DISTRICT COURT
MIDDLE DISTRICT OF TENN.
APR - 1 2010

RECEIVED
IN CLERK'S OFFICE
APR - 1 2010
U.S. DISTRICT COURT
MID. DIST. TENN.

BY_____
DEPUTY CLERK

DR. AYMAN AL-ZAWAHIRI;
JONATHAN LEE RICHES;
PLAINTIFF'S

V.

BONNAROO MUSIC & ARTS FESTIVAL;
DAVE MATTHEWS BAND;
BONNAROO.COM;
KINGS OF LEON;
STEVIE WONDER;
JAY-Z A/K/A SHAWN CARTER;
DEFENDANT'S

3:10mc50

PRELIMINARY INJUNCTION, TEMPORARY RESTRAINING ORDER

COMES NOW, THE PLAINTIFF'S DR. AYMAN AL-ZAWAHIRI AND JONATHAN LEE RICHES, WE FACE IMMINENT DANGER AND BODILY HARM FROM THE DEFENDANT's . WE MOVE FOR A RESTRAING ORDER AGAINST THEIR UPCOMING FESTIVAL BECAUSE THEIR MUSIC OFFENDS US AND IS IN VIOLATION OF ISLAMIC LAW. THEIR MUSIC IS A CIVIL RIGHTS VIOLATION TO US BECAUSE THEY OFFEND MUSLIMS IN THEIR LYRICS AND DEGRADE WOMEN. ALSO DEFENDAT'S PROMOTE THE SALE AND DISTRIBUTION OF ALCOHAL TO MINORS AS PLAINTTIFF'S THEMSELVES ARE RECOVERING ADDICTS AND THEIR CONCERT COULD TRIGGER US TO RELAPSE. WE PRAY THIS HONORABLE COURT WILL GRANT OUR RESTRAINING ORDER FOR RELIEF.

RESPECTFULLY,

_____ 03-26th-10
DR. AYMAN AL-ZAWAHIRI
PO BOX 14500
LEXINGTON, KY 40512

_____ 3-26-2010
JONATHAN LEE RICHES
40945-018
PO BOX
14500
LEXINGTON, KY 40512

In the United States District Court
For the Middle District of Tennessee

Jesse James,
Plaintiff

RECEIVED
APR 22 2010
U.S. DISTRICT COURT
MIDDLE DISTRICT OF TENN

CASE NO:

v.

Sandra Bullock;
Janine Lindemulder;
Jonathan Lee Riches;
Defendants

Preliminary Injunction, Temporary Restraining Order, TRO
28 USC 1331

Comes Now the Plaintiff, Jesse James, in pro-se, moves this honorable court to issue a restraining order against the Defendants who are threatening to kill me and ruin my reputation. I face imminent danger and bodily harm in Nashville and throughout Tennessee. Sandra Bullock seeks revenge on me and has been sleeping with multiple men to influence them to come and attack me on my motorcycle and to burn my businesses down. I found out through photographs that Defendant Bullock has been sleeping with Tiger Woods 69 times in March 2010, at a Nashville Super 8 motel and Bullock stole my Harley and drove to Aspen to cheat on me with Charlie Sheen and Bullock slept with Sen. John Edwards at a Charollette Bobcats basketball game and Bullock was sleeping with Keanu Reeves on a greyhound bus and she slept with Janine Lindemulder and Billy Ray Cyrus in a Dolly world restroom in Tennessee. Bullock had secret affairs on me with Eliot Spitzer at Niagrah Falls New York and she slept with Brad Pitt at Mardi Gras in New Orleans. Bullock secretly had mechanics to install toyota gas pedals on my motorcycles to make me crash and to crash Ben Rothesburger from Pittsburgh because of his anti-women behaviors. The Defendants cause me nightmares, Bullock tried to assault me with Michelle McGee's tatoo guns to give me Hep-C, and Bullock hired outlaw motorcycle gang members to pull a hit out on my life.

PAGE 3
James v. Bullock

The Defendants continue to defame my name and reputation. Defendant Bullock uses her salary to hire convicted Identity theft Kingpin Jonathan Lee Riches to hack into my finances and steal my credit cards and to illegally wiretap and listen to all my phone calls without my consent. Bullock also paid MR. Riches hundreds of thousands of dollars to post pictures of me sleeping with various women in other lawsuits that Riches is filing and talking about me and putting damaging evidence against me in the filing lawsuits that can be viewed online if you go to Justia.com and put in Jonathan Lee Riches or Google Jonathan Lee Riches or Google the following lawsuits: "Riches v. Swine flu", "Riches v. convicted child molesters", "Riches v. Courtney Love", "Riches v. The Twilight Zone", "Riches v. Beavis and Butt-head", "Riches v. Hulk Hogan", "Riches v. Justin Timberlake", "Riches v. Ecoli", "Riches v. Bullock", "Riches v. I can't believe its not Butter", "Riches v. 202-456-1414", "Riches v. Creative Artists Agency", "Riches v. Jay-z", "Riches v. The Academy Awards", "Riches v. Drew Brees", "Riches v. Combs", "Riches v. Daytona 500", "Riches v. Spears", "Riches v. Lohan", "Riches v. Aniston", "Riches v. Gotti", "Riches v. Eric Rudolph", "Riches v. Obama", "Riches v. Somali pirates", "Riches v. Lil Wayne", "Riches v. Hurricane Ike" — Go on Hurricane Ike lawsuit and see the end picture, "Riches v. Oprah Winfrey". I'm so scared of Jonathan Lee Riches, he has secret evidence against me that he is threatening to sell to the National Enquirer with pictures of me sleeping with Paris Hilton in Hilton head south carolina at a Hiltons, and having sexual contact with Megan Fox at 6 flags over Arlington and with me sleeping with Domestic Diva Martha Stewart with a Apron at her turkey hill ranch. I'm scared these photos will ruin my career. Also Riches claims he has evidence of my tax fraud at my west coast choppers buisness. I have nightmares of the Defendants. I seek a restraining order against them.

respectfully submitted

Jesse James
4-20-10

Jesse James
4-20-10

JUN 23 2010
U.S. DISTRICT COURT
EASTERN DISTRICT OF MO
ST. LOUIS

Jonathan Lee Riches a/k/a
Lionel Messi a/k/a
Diego Maradona,
Plaintiff

CASE NO:

v.

2010 World Cup a/k/a 2010 FIFA World Cup; Landon Donovan; Cristiano Ronaldo; Wayne Rooney; Team USA; Bob Bradley; Demarcus Beasley; Edson Buddle; Jozy Altidore; Clint Dempsey; Michael Bradley; Ricardo Clark; Steve Cherundolo; Oguchi Cherundolo; Jay Demerit; Tim Howard; Oguchi Onyewu; Carlos Bocanegra; Herculez Gomez; Stuart Holden; Jose Torres; Maurice Edu; Robbie Findley; Benny Feilhaber; Brad Guzan; Marcus Hahnemann; Jonathan Spector; Jonathan Bornstein; Clarence Goodson; Major League Soccer; Los Angeles Galaxy; Joe Gaetjens; David Beckham; English Premiere League; Confederations Cup; UEFA Champions League; Suweto's Orlando Stadium; England; Ashley Cole; Fabio Capello; Steven Gerrard; Algeria; Madjid Bougherra; Slovenia; African Nations Cup; Peter Osaze Odemwingie; Bafana Bafana; Georgios Samaras; Chicharito; Yoann Gourcuff; France; Uruguay; Thierry Henry; Nicolas Anelka; Franck Ribery; Diego Forlan; Argentina; Park Ji-Sung; Carlos Tevez; Nigeria; South Korea; Javier Mascherano; Greece; Dani Alves; Luis Fabiano; Didier Drogba; Brazil; Albertin Montoya; Portugal; Abby Wambach; Ivory Coast; Univision; Alex Frei; North Korea; Telefutura; Vicente del Bosque; Honduras; Iker Casillas; Carles Puyol; Switzerland; Cesc Fabregas; Spain; Xabi Alonso; Fernando Torres; Sebastion Pinera; Italy; Gianluigi Buffon; Ryan Nelsen; Fabio Cannavaro; Slovakia; New Zealand; Robert Vittek;

Salvador CABANAS; Paraguay; Arjen ROBBEN; Cameroon; Wesley Sneijder; Robin van Persie; Netherlands; Samuel Eto'o; Nicklas Bendtner; Denmark; Japan; Shunsuke Nakamura; Lukas Podolski; Germany; Miroslav Klose; Nemanja Vidic; Serbia; Tim Cahill; Serbia; Ghana; Bastian Schweinsteiger; Australia; Philipp Lahm; Soccer.com, Defendants

> Preliminary Injunction, Temporary Restraining order, TRO
> 28 USC 1331

Comes now, Jonathan Lee Riches a/k/a Lionel Messi d/b/a Diego Maradona. I face imminent danger and Bodily harm from the Defendants. I seek a restraining order.

The RDAP 500 Hour, Residential drug Abuse Program at the Federal Medical center in Lexington Kentucky is ran unconstitutional and I demand a Government investigation into their illegal Practices. This includes Mental, Emotional, Psychological, sexual Abuses inflicted on me and other RDAP Participants. RDAP engages in intimidation, Discrimination, Prejudice, corruption of RDAP staff which puts my life, the safety of the institution and other inmates lives in Jeopardy. The RDAP Program at FMC Lexington is ran by DR. Kristen Hungness. She needs to be arrested and investigated. DR. Hungness is currently having an Affair with another inmate in the RDAP program named Robert Annaheim. Robert Annaheim also got DR. Hungness Pregnant in 2009, and they have a child together. DR. Hungness has cocaine, Herion, and Needles stored in her office which is located in the veritas unit basement. Another Drug Treatment Specialist member is named DR. Amanda Hughes a/k/a DR. Amanda Leigh Hughes. She is the Mastermind behind the corruption in the program. DR. Hughes is having a current Relationship which is sexual with Patrick J. Simpson, #05095-036. DR Hughes has had sex with him over 100 times in her office located in the basement of the Veritas unit, in Staff Alley during DR. Hughe's late Night every Wednesday Night around 8:30pm after NA (Narcotics Anonymous). DR. Hughes has illegally smuggled Narcotics including Marajuana, oxycotin, cocaine, herion, Needles, HGH, PCP, Diuretics, morphine into the prison hidden in her body cavity, her purse in which she uses the Drugs with Patrick Simpson and Simpson sells the Drugs through out the Prison for Profit for him and DR Amanda Hughes. DR Hughes drives to prison Different nights of the week and throws Packages of drugs over the Perimeter Fence into the recreation Yard where Patrick Simpson retrieves it and sells. Patrick Simpson hides the contraband in the chapel where he works as a clerk. DR. Hughes smuggled in Cell Phones for Simpson, so Simpson can use to call DR. Hughes at home at night, to make Gambling bets, drug buys. Simpson speaks to un-indicted co-defendants of his discussing revenge murder plots on victims, to finance his terrorist views. DR. Hughes also provides MR. Simpson Access to her work computer so they both view Internet Pornography, child porn, Place sports bets, look up all information on search Engines. Rick Dooley is another Drug treatment specialist who is embezzling funds. Dooley is stealing Government documents and taking them home. Rick Dooley has sex with Animals, he has Addictions and vices including Possessing Pornography of little boys stored on his work computer in Veritas. Rick Dooley uses his Phone at work to call 1-900 Gay Phone sex lines while on his lunch Break and Arranges to meet middle school boys afterwork each week at local Lexington Kentucky Burger Kings, and McDonalds, Buying the boys happy meals in exchange for oral sex. Rick Dooley also has a male Blowup doll in his cabinets in his office and I have his DNA on a used condom I got from his garbage can in his office.

Ms. Mattingly looks like Porky Pig, she constantly eats, she eats prison food from food service without paying, she brings her purse and stuffs it with Rolls, milk cartons, then takes it home. This is theft of Government Property.

Dr. Natalie Riley is color blind, she also solicits sex in her office with other inmates. Dr. Riley has been cheating on her husband since 2008. Dr. Riley snorts cocaine on her Desk in her office. Dr. Riley uses her computer and masterbates to animal pornography she is involved in Beastiality. Dr. Riley is involved with the mexican Drug cartels. Dr. Riley smuggles narcotics across the Rio Grande in her panties which she wears for a week straight without changing. Dr. Riley is HIV Positive and she has numerous sexually transmitted diseases which she spreads when she does covert Prostitution at night in the Red Light District of Lexington Kentucky. Dr. Riley cheats on her IRS taxes, she is in Debt to the Columbians and to the Gambino crime family. Dr. Riley wears a wedding ring which was stolen through a Jewelery Heist. Dr. Riley dresses up as a man Catholic Priest during each Halloween and molests little boys. Dr. Riley is the one who Kidnapped and killed JonBenet Ramsey with Rick Dooley as a accomplice. Dr. Riley injects illegal drugs in her Arms at veritas in her office, she steals the morphine and methadone from the FMC Lexington Pharmacy

Dr. Riley has had sex with every single prison male guard at FMC Lexington at least twice each. Dr. Riley has major sex addictions. If you google Dr. Natalie Riley you can see her masterbating to fruits and vegetables in her office. Dr. Riley assaulted a nun and plays the video on Youtube.com. Dr. Riley sells drugs to kids in school zones. Dr. Riley injects heroin in her arms, dumps the used needles on public beaches. Dr. Riley shop lifts sex toys from Adam & Eve shops. Dr. Riley is racist, she has Hitler and Nazi tatoos all across her body. Dr. Riley attends Klu Klux Klan meetings, she is in the Kentucky Militia. Dr. Riley plead alegence to Al-queda. Dr. Riley sneaks around Elderly Peoples windows at night and peeps and flashes disabled people. Dr. Riley goes to gas station pumps and sniffs fumes at BP stations. Dr. Riley spray painted Nazi signs at Jewish Synagogues. I seen Dr. Riley kidnap dogs and cats and abuses, tortures them and hangs them. Dr. Riley is a Anti-Jew also. She assaults numerous Blacks, Jews, Koreans randomly. Dr. Riley kidnapped a little African American girl selling Girl Scout cookies, Riley raped her in the woods, then tied a noose around her head and hung her, branding a Nazi sign on her forehead. Dr. Riley is clearly out of control. Dr. Riley molests boys with Autism. Dr. Riley embezeled meals on wheels profit. Dr. Riley sleeps with bums on street corners in Skid Row Los Angeles. Dr. Riley uses her federal pay check to donate to Hezbollah and Al-queda churches. In Dr. Riley's spare time she vandalizes war veterans grave stones, kicking them over. Dr. Riley set california wild fires, she burns Black chwrchs.

Dr. Riley has black slaves working on her Plantation. Dr. Riley also grows Marijuana and Poppy seeds in her back yard and Dr. Riley has a meth lab in her basement. Dr. Riley donates her HIV blood to the United Way. Dr. Riley parks in handicap zones, Dr. Riley had a secret sex change operation. Dr. Riley stole Dr. Hurgness's capital one no hassles card to get Breast implants and Dr. Riley is a convicted felon. She robs Kroger stores, shoplifts from white castle Hamburgers. Dr. Riley wears a wig, Dr. Riley has sex with Politians, she films it. Dr. Riley and the whole RDAP community needs to get investigated. I will sue RDAP staff forever to stop them from torturing me, torturing other inmates creating Havoc on my life. I lost my hopes and dreams. I came out of treatment worse then I came in. I saw Dr. Riley urinate on the U.S. Constitution on July 4th. On christmas, Dr. Riley Assaulted Santa Claus at a Public Mall and she stole the Salvation Arm kettle to buy steroids and pay off her gambling debts. I'm so scared of RDAP I move for a Restraining order. Each of the Defendants know the abuse RDAP is inflicting on me but won't stop it. The Defendants are aiding and abetting RDAP and their staff. If this court Don't help me I will die. I pray for relief.

respectfully

6-15-10

Jonathan Lee Riches
#40448018
Federal Medical Center
P.O. Box 14500
Lexington, KY 40512
859-255-6812

<u>Complaint Addendum</u>

I, Jonathan Lee Riches also state the following Criminal Acts that the World Cup of 2010, the defendants, Previous world cups, Stanley cups, Cups of tea have commited on my life like Major Psychological damage and Identity theft, Acts of Genocide towards me and people in the witness protection Plan.

Since Feb, 26th 2003, I'm being discriminated by the Defendants from Entering and Participating in the 2010 World cup. I'm a 15 time All american soccer superstar, All Purpose utility man. I can play every Position. The Great Pele was my teacher since Grade School. I'm a citizen of the Isle of Mann, Isle of Jersey off the British channel Islands, Its a off-shore Tax Haven. I'm part of a fraud dream team of convicted felon soccer Players. On my team is: Bernard Madoff, Jeff Skilling, Bernied Ebbers, John Rigas, Michael Milken, TJX Hacker Alberto Gonzales, Gov. Blagojevich, Conrad Black, Former Gov. Eddie Edwards of Louisanna, Super Hacker Kevin Mitnick, and Quest CEO Joseph Nacchio. We been practicing together for 4 years in the Bureau of Prisons rec Yard. We Also played Kick the can on 1-12-09. We plan on being a International traveling team of Identity thieves where we all get out of Prison. I'm working on all their Appeals. I have Evidence Posh spice Ate Cristiano Ronaldo's Soccer Ball behind David Beckham's Back on Valentines day. FIFA President Sepp Blatter denied us entry to play in the 2010 world cup in Africa. Sepp Blatter Also gave me bladder cancer. I sued David Beckham, Riches v. Beckham. The Defendants are in a Major conspiracy. All of them stole Wilson from Tom Hanks on castaways. then the Defendants have been providing militants in Gaza soccer balls to throw at Israelis over the Berlin wall. Defendants are collectively the mess. For instance, England Goalie Robert Green was caught with BP oil on his hands when Dempsey kicked the ball in the goal and slipped away from Greene. Greene was making a political statement to go Green and not depend of foreign oil. Paraguay Goalie did the same thing but Justo Villar did not pay when he pulled up to a St. Louis BP station, got 87 octane, drove off without paying $11.23 Bill. The Defendants are involved in Game fixing, shaving points, and illegal sports betting with Duke lacrosse Players. The 2010 World cup hired former NBA ref Tim Donaghy, Pete Rose, Umpire Jim Joyce, MLB ump Joe West, and NFL Guy Ed Hulociko be refs using my stolen Identity on 9/11/1 to get zebra outfits from S. African illegal Poaching. Then Tim Howard Goalie of the US is in a conspiracy with Chili's Bar and Grill, as now Mr. Howard has a Endorsement contract with Chili's Baby back ribs. Give me my baby back, Give me my baby back. I scored 12 goals Against Dwight Howard on the Howard Stern show against Buckwheat. Then in the 4th grade I kicked a Soccer Ball across the Potomic. I got secret Information about JaBulani Soccer Ball. We at the Federal Medical Center in lexington at the UNICOR program are forced in sweat shop labor to make 2010 world cup soccer balls. we are being whipped and chained by Cool Hand Luke. A week before the world cup we were forced to make 52,000 Soccer Balls within 2 hours, and one lucky soccer ball inside has a Golden ticket to willy wonka's chocolate factory. We then sent all the Inmate made JuBulani soccer Balls to QVC, where defendants bought them in bulk under my Identity and cap. to one No hassel card. I'm on the worlds Endangered Species List, I'm one of a Kind. South Africans gave me aids, Desmond Tutu and Mandela Blew out my ear drums with VuVu Zelas on Defendants special orders. I sued South Africa. Riches v. South Africa and Riches v. Black history month, Riches v. Jena 6 ; Defendants all forced me to wear their used mouthpieces. This is my mea culpa, I admit

I'm powerless over my Addictions, If you look at lawsuit Riches v. Hurricane Ike, My Picture is as a exhibit, who is skinnier, me or Posh spice? The defendants are in a conspiracy with the North Korea dictator, Inside each world cup soccer Balls are Nuclear Secrets and bags of uncle Bens rice to supply the North's troops. Defendants paid Michigan state coach Tom Izzo to sodomize me with Nikes at a Cleveland cavs game in 2008. Then the Defendants for fun told Michaele Salahi, Tareq Salahi to crash my Parole hearing. The 2006 world cup was played in my back Yard, Defendants Tore my Grass, stepped in my Garden, Littered, Stole my fathers chainsaw then I got molested by the Defendants at a Peewee Soccer also by Peewee who stole my Bike - given it me by Floyd Landis, hid in 10 Alamo Rent-A-Car- they carJacked Ko Jack with a Lojack, Jackie chan I was Assaulted by the Michlen Man. I can Juggle soccer Balls and write lawsuits at the same time. Defendants gave me shin splints, 1800-Hairline-for-men fractures, Japanese Joe Jam, Tonya Harding Busted my knee at the 2010 world cup try-outs. I was dressed as a Soccer mom, I personally injected Hgh and Steroids into each defendant, they lined up for hot soup, the economy is bad. Ronaldo has secret Affairs with Kelly Osbourne. Me and Landon Donovan are involved in a current lawsuit and Appeal. Weymouth v. Riches, appeal #10-5338 and the case is U.S. District court E.D. of Kentucky case # 5: 2010 CV 00056. I was a white farmer Mandela worked on my Plantation, I file this suit before the world cup ends, The winner Plans to use my head as a trophey, I'm scared, The Defendants then plan to experiment and use my head for the 2014 world cup and Willis need to take my leg. BP energy Giant sponsors the Entire

ISSUE 10   World cup, Landon Donovan worked on the Deepwater horizon rig part time in the off season and Hugo Chavez sold him a defaulty blow out preventer on ebay. Chavez64 was the seller. The Taliban plan to enter the 2014 world cup bribing the Salt Lake city Olympic committee option to enter. A one legged soccer man killed Richard Kimball. Defendants sent me to Alaska made me put my tongue on a frozen soccer post. Ralphie shot me with a red Rider BB Gun. I stole Scott Furkas' Identity bought the defendants cocaine and oxycotin off Rush Limbaugh's CVS drug store perscription. Defendants are forging my signature and signing soccer balls for fans and are advertizing my Jonathan Lee Riches Jersey next to Kobe Bryants at foot locker and Soccer.com stole Mia Hamms Bra I bought from Namar at a Boston garage sale. Read lawsuits. Riches v. Alice in Wonderland, Riches v. Kobe Bryant, Riches v. Starwars, Riches v. Abdulmutallab, Riches v. American Idol, Riches v. Lifestyles of the Richard famous. I seek restraining orders and Steroiding testing for all the Defendants, DNA testing, cheek swabs, urine testing. Landon Donovan has Floyd Landis, Barry Bonds, Jose Canseca, Tim Montgomery, and Balco founder Victor Conti's phone numbers in his cell phone. Why is Donovan calling these felons. Riches v. Conti, Riches v. Giambi, Riches v. Dykstra. I pray this Court for relief.

respectfully

6-17-10

Jonathan Lee Riches
#40948018
Federal Medical Center
Lexington, KY 40512
859-255-6812

EASTERN DISTRICT OF MISSOURI

Jonathan Lee Riches a/k/a
Aubrey Drake Graham,
Plaintiff

CASE NO:

V.

Justin Bieber,
Taylor Swift,
Miley Cyrus,
Greyson Chance,
Defendant's

Preliminary Injunction, Temporary Restraining order, TRO
28 USC 1331

Comes now, the Plaintiff, Jonathan Lee Riches a/k/a Aubrey Drake Graham, I face imminent danger and bodily harm. The four defendants are my children and I'm seeking custody of them. If this Court does not intervene and save my children, they will become Endangered Species. I want DNA testing, I fathered the four children, I have Justin Biebers hair, Taylor swifts nose, Miley Cyrus ears and Greyson Chance belly button. These Defendants are in danger from Adult Pedophiles and celebrity Stalkers. I seek custody from each of them. I can provide the Defendants with 24 hour security at the Federal Medical center in Lexington Kentucky, with Armed guard services surrounding Barb wire fencing to keep prey away from my babies. I can provide the Defendants with 3 square meals a day including milk in the morning so their Bones grow. I can provide the Defendants with universal Government health care. The Prison library can meet the defendants Educational needs. I want to be a father I always dreamed I could be. Each night the defendants can sit on my lap and I can read them Bed time stories uninterrupted. Then in my cell. I have 1 blanket but we can cover up like a tent. I can read them Spin magazines and the Prison TV's show Bet & Mtv so we can Rock! We have a huge rec Yard. I can play horeshoes with the defendants or we could go to the hobby and craft shop and make prison Art so we could send to their Grandmother in Pennsylvania which is my Mommy. If the Defendants stay with me they will be safe from Paparottzi and the prison commissary sells Halls cough drops so they wont lose their voice. We have decks of cards here so we can play spades for push ups and the rec Yard has a weight pile. I want Justin Bieber to get Buff like me. Justin Bieber is my hero and I'm very proud of his sucess which I taught him how to sing at Westboro Baptist church at Veterans funerals. I met Justin Biebers mother Pattie Mallette on Eharmony.com and got her pregnant outside Bad Boy records in New York city. I financed Def Jam Music Group with Identity theft in my criminal case. Me and Bieber are going to start a new record label "Identity theft Jam". Justin Bieber is already going Bald. Bieber illegally used my capital one no hassel credit card to get a hair club for men, and strawberry shortcake hair dye at CVS Pharmacy. If I don't get custody of Miley Cyrus fast, I'm affraid my nemisis Warren Jeffs is going to marry her in Utah or Hannah Montana. I intercepted a phone call where former NFL Player Lawrence Taylor was trying to meet Miley Cyrus at a Orlando super 8 motel. Taylor Swift was born on John Kerrys swift Boat. Ellen Degeneres is trying to make Greyson Chance a women with my credit cards. The Defendants mean everything to me. I paid a prison tatoo artist 100 packs of mackeral to have the defendants images on my forearms and I smuggled in the Defendants Posters to hang above my Bunk. When I hear the Defendants on the radio I get goose bumps and cry, they are special and they are a part of my heart. I saved my Daughter Taylor Swift a few months ago from Nashville floods. Then I found out that the Defendants, my children are getting psychologically

Brainwashed By psychologist Dr. Amanda Hughes a/k/a Dr. Amanda Leigh Hughes, Drug Treatment specialist at the RDAP, residential Drug abuse program at the Federal medical center in Lexington Kentucky. The Defendants meet with Dr. Hughes collectively every monday and wednesday at 12:50pm in Dr. Hughes small group. Dr. Hughes is encouraging the Defendants to smoke pot in School zones, shoot cocaine at Rock concerts like Led Zepplin and Britney Spears Tours and the Defendants are encouraged to have unprotected sex with foreigners and Dr. Hughes is teaching my kids how to make suicide Bomber vests so they can Blow up themselves and crowds at their concerts. Dr. Hughes is Showing The Defendants Animal pornography at Disneys Animal Kingdom. Dr. Hughes gives the Defendants ecstacy to Attend Raver Paul oakenfold raves, my kids are going to die before they are 25. This worries me as a Parent. Dr. Hughes tells the Defendants to drink and drive without seat belts and to shoplift with winnona Ryder at Saks 5th ave. Dr. Hughes has been using the Defendants as guinea Pigs with Drug experiments in her office in a Dark Basement in the veritas Unit, I'm scared. I saw Taylor swift on the country music channel with needle marks in her right arm. Dr. Hughes also told Taylor Swift to have sex with Billy Ray Cyrus at Nickelodeon Studios. Justin Bieber stole my American Express to get a Penis Enlargement on Dr. Amanda Hughes direct orders, The peoples Greatest Frustrations with me is also my Greatest strength. I keep Bloggers and public glued to their computers each day Enquiring about my suits, and having them contemplate my meanings and motives. "Is Jun insane, or is it a con game, like whats in Barry Bonds veigns" I can walk into Belgium with a Islamic veil and people would think I'm a women, or a ninja. The Defendants took my Brains from my smart Phone, replaced t with a Dumb Phone with Down syndrom. I was Batmans Butler. My Pet dog was buried at Stephen Kings Pet cemetary. I sued American Idol. see <u>Riches v. American Idol</u>

Defendants sent William Refrigerator Perry to eat what is left of me. The Beatles put Bugs on my Prison Floor and Volkswagen. Beyonce put me in a halo. The Defendants are under Alot of Stress and anxiety. Justin Bieber is developing Acne and hemmoruids and Greyson chance has been defying Puberty. John Mark Karr tried to take the defendants to Thailand with David Caradine and Justin Bieber is getting singing lessons from milli vanilli and Taylor Swift. The Defendants each slept with Michael Jackson at the Neverland when they were 12. Rocker Tommy Lee made a sex tape with each defendant behind Pamela's BACK. Taylor Swift secretly got Sodomized with a grammy by Kanye West in a chicago Alley. Defendants and Lady Gaga gave me the finger at epcot center. Justin Bieber was R Kellys secret lover. Justin Bieber lost his virginity to madonna. Greyson chance is in a Secret Relationship with Lance Bass. Taylor swift Licked Lil waynes Lollipop at the Bet music Awards. The Defendants are headed for Death and Destruction. Bieber already told me he wants to be like Kurt Cobain and Jimmy Morrison. I need custody of the Defendants. I get Nightmares and Panic Attacks knowing the whole world are corrupting them like society did to me. I'm afraid Justin Bieber will want to be Just Like me, his father and give up music to be a International identity thief. I'm in the Guinessbook of World records for stealing the most Identities in the history of mankind. I can be reached or contacted at the below Address I'm open to all Media interviews with reporters or Bloggers. I move for a restraining order to stop the Defendants from performing, Singing and producing music. I seek immediate custody. I pray for relief.

Respectfully

7-20-10

Jonathan Lee Riches
#40945018
Federal Medical Center
P.O. Box 14500
Lexington, KY 40512
859-255-6812

District of ARIZONA
TUCSON DIVISION

Julian Assange a/k/a
Jonathan Lee Riches,
Plaintiff

CASE NO.

v.

CW11-59 TUC DCB

Jared Lee Loughner a/k/a
Jared Loughner a/k/a
Mumtaz Qadri,
Defendant

Preliminary Injunction, Temporary Restraining order
TRO
28 USC 1331

I face imminent danger and Bodily harm from the Defendant Jared Lee Loughner. I was personally effected and traumatized by the Defendants actions which are inexcusable and my thoughts and Prayers go out to the victims including U.S. Rep Gabrielle Giffords, chief Judge John Roll, Christina-Taylor Green and the Entire Tucson community. Now I'm in fear of the Defendant in which he is in federal custody and I want a restraining order against him preventing the Bureau of Prisons from transfering the Defendant to the federal Medical Center in Lexington Kentucky where the Defendant will recieve a mental health evaluation on his criminal case, and I'm in fear that if the Defendant transfers to FMC Lexington he will be placed in solitary confinement where I'm currently being illegally detained and possibly being my cell mate in which he could use his bare hands or a prison shank to kill me for being a moderate democrat and for me Jonathan Lee Riches being in the Guiness book of world rewards for suing the most people in the history of mankind and for me being a extreme High profile inmate. I'm illegally serving over a decade in federal prison for being a ringleader in a international identity theft conspiracy along with computer hacking, phishing, spamming with wire fraud via cyberwarfare with Botnets and Trojan horses stealing the personal information of millions of internet service providers customers. See U.S. v. Riches, Case # 4-03-90 S.D. of Texas. I'm a federal whistleblower on Government corruption and physical, sexual, and mental abuse within the federal prison system in which to silence me I'm been in solitary confinement for over a year, and the government plans to indict me on new federal charges of forgery or fraud for filing lawsuits exposing corruption to keep me in prison past March 23, 2012 which is my release date. Now the Government also filed a civil preliminary injunction against me, preventing me from filing anymore lawsuits and giving the Bureau of Prisons Authorization to open up my sealed legal mail and return it to me without being sent through the mail. See U.S. v. Riches Case # 5:10-CV-00322 KSF, which is violating my constitutional rights to the courts. I'm in solitary, and continue to get physically, mentally and sexually abused by Dr. Kristen Hungness, Dr. Amanda Leigh Hughes, Warden Deborah Hickey, SIA Mary Anderson, Officer Howe, etc. Al. I had to smuggle this lawsuit out of the prison, otherwise FMC Lexington would of threw it away, even though I put a stamp on it, which is mail fraud on their part. In order to get this lawsuit out, I arranged with a Army of Ants which are scattered on my floor. I put bread crumbs in the top of this envelope and at least 10,000 ants carried this lawsuit in the backs and marched it outside under the Emergency exit, from this point I arranged with a few pigeons I've been communicating with via sign language to pick up the lawsuits from the ants and fly it personally to the courthouse doorsteps in Tucson Arizona since the pigeons have to fly south for the winter anyway. I figure since the pigeons hit the jet stream it will expedite the delivery process, and this lawsuit will hit the courts by the end of January 2011 a few weeks after the mass shooting that Defendant Jared Lee Loughner committed. Jared Loughner was also personally influenced weeks before by Mumtaz Qadri in Pakistan. The Safeway grocery store is suppose to be safe, all safeways need to get Lifelock. Defendant Loughner took a taxi to Safeway driven by Robert Dinero who escaped from Cape Fear, and the taxi had 4 sets of Firestones bought at El Campo tires where Gabrielle Giffords once worked. El Campo tires also provided tires to Jim Leyritz, Gov of South Dakota,

Lisa "Lefteye" Lopez, Dale Earnhardt SR, Andrew Gallo, Richie Valens, and Brayton Edwards. The 9mm Glock Nine Defendant Loughner had was given to him by Cho at Virginia Tech who he got from the Columbine Kids where they got the WMD's from Suddam Hussein, Defendant Jared is also friends with Jared from Subway, a 6 inch Submarine. When I heard of the Tucson Tragedy, I made a flag out of Prison toilet paper and flew it at ½ stance, then on 1-10-11, I had a 11am Eastern moment of silence for the victims but I was interrupted by other Afro-American inmates in solitary cells banging and Hollering because we didn't get served fried chicken for lunch yet, I believe "Congress at Your Corner" was set up by U.S. Rep Gabrielle Giffords to expose and repeal tough Federal Sentencing guidelines and Giffords was planning to expose my illegal incarceration and the violation of my 8th amendment rights for cruel and unusual punishment at 10:20am, but Loughner prevented her from speaking about my case to make the world aware of me, I nominate Roger Salzgeber, Bill Badger, and Joseph Zamudio for a congressional medal of honor and to try out for tackles for the Arizona Cardinals. Patricia Maisch is also a hero, and I personally propose to her. Gabrielle Giffords husband Mark Kelly is a NASA Astronaught and I believe, if Barack Obama releases more federal funding to the space program, Mark Kelly could fly into space on Feb. 8, 2011 exactly 1 light month away from Earth with a super sensitive telescope from the Sharper Image with a Laser Beam and zoom in on Tucson at 9:59 am and he could Beam the light into Loughners eyes to blind him, So this tragedy would be prevented. Now federal tax payers will suffer because their pocket change will have to pay for all members of congress security and all the FBI Agents that are in Tucson will build a permanent command center for extra manpower to stop illegal immigration over the border. This tragedy flooded the am networks with Breaking news and Regular schedule programming on Sean Hannity, Mark Levin, coast to coast with George Nore was interrupted and the Am radio is the only outside news source I have in solitary. The Defendants Actions also made me cry. I seek a restraining order against him.

Submitted

Jonathan Lee Riches 1/11/11
#40948018
Federal Medical Center
P.O. Box 14500
Lexington, KY 40512
859-255-6812

Jonathan Lee Riches d/b/a
Ali Hassan Al-Majid a/k/a
Kat Stacks,
Plaintiff

v.

"Don't ask, Don't Tell"; Gay Marriage; Proposition 8;
Gay Pride Parade; Nudist Colony; Swingers Club;
Sexual Transmitted diseases; Chaz Bono; Liz Cheney;
YMCA; Harvey Milk; Lesbians; Homosexuals; Samantha
Ronson; Barney Frank; HIV a/k/a Human Immuno deficiency
Virus; The Village People; Linda Lovelass; Tyson Gay;
Full Metal Jacket; Rainbow Floats; National Center for
Lesbian Rights; Employment Non-discrimination Act,
Defendants

Preliminary Injunction, Temporary Restraining Order, TRO
28 USC 1331

Comes now, Jonathan Lee Riches d/b/a Ali Hassan Al-Majid (Chemical Ali) a/k/a Kat Stacks, in Pro-se, I and the American People along with worldwide Heterosexuals and Virgins face imminent danger and bodily harm from "Don't ask, Don't tell" and the conspirator of Defendants.

This is a Gigantic fraud of Epic porportions which endangers me, endangered species, the defendants undermine our Korans and Bibles perverting the world with filth, which the defendants will ruin marriages, corrupt children and morals/values will be eliminated. Our Forefathers would be rolling in their graves sick, Foreign Terrorists with use the Defendants for justification for Holly wars, Anarcists will street protest, cyber criminals will launch computer viruses Nuns will rebel.

"Don't ask, Don't tell" is a psychological trap. I don't care if you tell or not but all forms of Homosexuality is wrong. I was forced to eat at TGI Fridays with Gay waiters serving me. The Defendants plan to start Martial Law and all Heterosexual marriages nationwide will be annulled, American curves magazines will be banned. Chaz Bono is going to be Times Person of the Year. Then Somali Pirates of the Carribean will demand man booty for ransom. Our 4 branches of the military plan to convert all other militarys, insurgencies, narco-drug traffickers world wide into Homosexuals to ruin global growth in populations and male prostitution will be at all military bases. At Ft. Bragg, male soldiers will brag to each other how big their penis's are. The military will label Homophobia a mental illness. At the Gay Pride Parade all soldiers will swing dance on rootbeer floats. Hasbro will sell Gay GI-Joe Action figures. Then our troops coming home from duty with PTS will shoot all straight people for not loving them. The Army is building pink tanks, rainbow color airplanes. All our generals will be at central command watching Gay Porn. AT&T has plans to change its name to Gay T&T. My cell mate Bubba already proposed to me and he was in McCain's Navy. Uncle Sam is now dressed as a drag Queen, soldiers will give each other Hummers in their Hummers, our troops are teaching Afgans to come out of the closet. The village people plan to join the navy. Now at all military Barracks the Defendants caused male troops to have Ricky Martin Brad Pitt posters and now male troops Hobbies overseas are spin the bottle, duck, duck Goose, Trivia pursuit, knitting, painting each others toes, blasting music like Right Said Fred "I'm too sexy", "Macho Man", Madonna's "Borderline". Male soldiers plucking each others eyebrows, giving each other foot messages. I wanted to join the Marines when I got out of prison and to marry GI-Jane, but she went lesbian on me. Guantanamo Bay turned into a gay health spa. Now Bin Laden wears a pink turban, shaved his beard with Bikini wax. Homosexuals at Arlington cemetary will come out of their closets. John McCain slept with Pat Tillman. Boy George, George Michael, Harvey Milk and the Jonas Brothers plan to join the Airforce. Omaha Beach is a nudist colony. No male troops will sleep peaceful in their Barracks constant moaning and groaning. It will smell like poop, condom machines in the latrine. Robert E. Lee slept with Sherman at woodstock to negotiate peace. The Defendants must be stopped. I'm whistleblowing and will become a draft dodging AWOL in a underground bomb shelter under the Vatican away from Gay Catholic Priests too. I move for restraining orders.

respectfully

Jonathan Lee Riches 9/11/10
#40948018
Federal Medical Center
P.O. Box 14500
Lexington, KY 40512

Riches,
Plaintiff
v.
Lopez,
Defendant

5:07-CV-11458

MAY 29 2012
CLERK'S OFFICE
DETROIT

Notice of Appeal
Jonathan Lee Riches Appeals to the 6th Circuit Court of Appeals

I, Jonathan Lee Riches, Appeal. Jennifer Lopez put me in prison. I was her former boyfriend fiancee before Marc Anthony and I did millions of dollars in fraud with credit cards to finance Lopez's career. I bought her Saks 5th ave Bras, JC Penney's Leg warmers, and Sam Goody gift certificates to buy her own CD's to boost her record sales. Then I used stolen peoples identities to get Lopez Breast Implants, a tummy tuck worth $11,252.64 and Avon facial cream. Lopez manipulated me, and she abandoned me after I went to prison for 125 months. Lopez violated my copyrighted music, "Jenny from the Block" was my idea and while Lopez was married to Marc Anthony she cheated on Anthony with comedian George Lopez and former ATL MLB catcher Javier Lopez, I have the proof on video tape. Email me at Johnnysuenami@gmail.com I Appeal.

respectfully
5-20-12
Jonathan Lee Riches
143 Roebling St.
Suite 5
Brooklyn, NY 11211

Riches,
Plaintiff
v.
Pitt, et al
Defendants

2:07-CV-14615

FILED
MAY 29 2012
CLERK'S OFFICE
DETROIT

Notice of Appeal

Jonathan Lee Riches appeals the dismissal of this case to the 6th circuit court of Appeals

I am the real father to Bradd Pitt and Angelina Jolies children, all of them have my DNA, and they are forbidding me from taking a blood sample. I met Jolie on the set of Hackers, and I'm the real Johnny Lee that she married. Jolie used to make me put my finger in her mouth to be bulimic. Brad Pitt stole my credit cards on Fight club. I was molested by Brad Pitt on Sleepers. Brad Pitt and George Clooney broke into my piggy bank at my home in a oceans 11 plot. Pitt stole my cocaine stash I got from cheech n chong. Jolie and I were pen pals in prison. I got love letters of Jolie to produce to the courts as Evidence or email me at Johnnysuenami@gmail.com   I Appeal

respectfully   [signature]   5-22-12

Jonathan Lee Riches
143 Roebling St.
Suite S
Brooklyn, NY 11211

DISTRICT OF MONTANA

RECEIVED MAR 1 2016

Jonathan Lee Riches,
Plaintiff

CASE NO.

v.

Daylight Saving Time,
Defendants

Preliminary Injunction
Temporary Restraining Order, TRO

Comes Now, Jonathan Lee Riches, in pro-se, Moves this honorable court for a Restraining Order Against Daylight Saving Time, and for the clocks to move back to its original form.

I face Danger from Daylight Saving Time which is disrupting my biological clock, it Disrupts my sleeping patterns which could cause me to get a heart attack.

Daylight saving time disrupts all Americans farming, travel, record keeping, medical devices, Daylight Saving time is manipulating our Earths natural cycle, we dont need Government interference in our lives, this is a Danger.

Also, Daylight Saving time is misrepresenting and inaccurate, since no daylight is actually saved. It should be changed to Daylight Shifting time. If this court wont grant the restraining order in the Alternative, too much light will cause me skin cancer and extra vitamin D the Defendants are a Danger to children because it causes obesity in kids having extra daylight to go trick or treating during Halloween. Daylight Saving time Effects the bottom line of Radio stations who can only operate in the day. Also, it brings confusion to travelers and Residents of Hawaii, Parts of indiana, Guam, Puerto Rico who don't celebrate Daylight Saving time.

I seek a restraining order Against Daylight Savingtime - put the clocks back - the whole world needs to follow the same time - this will bring a togetherness in the world, cause the goal is to bring a new world order Anyway, so we need all the clocks the same. I am a Proud American facing danger because of this clock Atrocity - please help.

I pray for relief.

3/10/16

Respectfully

Jonathan Lee Riches
7001 Elmwood Ave
Philadelphia, PA 19142

Poems

It's a new day!
Let's see if I make the news today
From some of the suits I display
I'm like Uday, not Saddam's son,
But I'm Jon, mon,
And I'm litigating like a Jamaican rasta,
Call me J-Rock star
Odds are, none pissed the cops off more than JLR
Through the courts,
I use the force, the Luke of lawsuits,
Jon Han Solo,
I'm riding solo,
I'm the Jason Derulo of Litigation,
Numero uno!

Walked out the halfway house to go on a pass,
Beautiful day, then BAM! Giant gnat
Flew right into my eye, ruined my sky
I'm suin the city of Philadelphia
For violating the Clean Air Act
And bugging me!

Adam's pist about Travis the chimp
Shit shouldn't have happened
Crooked cops shootin animals for kicks
No remorse for this

On the flip side
Law enforcement sicks dogs on us all without resistin
I was once bitten
Kickin clawin by dogs jaws like I'm raw chicken
Mauled leavin me wit stitches
I'm a victim for bein Jonathan Lee Riches

I play hardball at litigation, they pitch softballs at my bat
Fact is my tactics is immaculate, I'm the switch hitter,
R.i.c.h.e.s make them shiver, my lawsuits bigger
Than the tallest bitterroot, cause I got the juice,
I'm the O.J. of pro-se! Whatchu say!

Say someone in a vehicle does you wrong
And you only got the license plate to go on.
Sue the license plate number, along

With the individual as "Doe, Jane/John."

Once the suit has been filed, free

Of charge for you because you proceed
Informa pauperis, then you petition the courts to
Have the DMV subpoenaed to release
The vehicle owner's name to you!

Bloody Sunday school, red dawn, bread gone, bled run bled run, meticulous exorcisms on kids, I'm devilish, God loves the smell of flesh, 666 victims inflictin flame wick, burnin fake Christians, bibles are liable for lies and fiction.

I'm the Law Paul Revere, if you look behind me,
You'll see all these crooks and tyranny
But I stay ahead of them,

Take Juan Valdez's horse to the courts, no settlin,

Get the recourse, me and my horse

Is a force in these courts, of course

Killen kids da illest, ask Albert Fish Tru brilliance
I'm lovin new villains
Getkicks offsickness
Mutha approved
Betta skip school or get pistol whipped
Refs wit a whistle
Blown on deaf ears
No protection your death nears
Executioner lucifer
Your text books no bullet proof vest I'm coo coo, clock time to glock em Reminds me of Cho '07 Virginia Tech Dissected flesh and I'm smilin
I'm appetizing for a dyin corpse

This shit a joke, but whatcha gon do? Revoke my
passes
For freedom of expression against oppressive fascists! Philly po-po's oh so
democratic,
Foes got me dependent off some whack shit! They say: I'm a
addict
        I behave like a manic I gotta
            pay taxes
                Gotta stay at this halfway shack, it's
                      the pits!

I just wish this shit would go away, fast quick!

Wholesome to me to see a shootin spree in an old folks home. Go postal by locos broke yo no social security. Anarchy in AARP. Hell to elderly. An end to retirement. You die by 65.

Today I woke up, broke as fuck,
And I can't even go get a donut.
So what? I'll just bust a nut

On Pornhub, for free, no more horny –

Now I can go after authority!

(photo of the plaintiff as a young man)

Special thanks goes to Elle Inez for her help in compiling the many lawsuits and letters that were reviewed for this book.

Michael Sajdak has written for F Newsmagazine and Thought Catalog, appeared in Hobart Literary Magazine and others. He lives in Chicago.

Printed in Poland
by Amazon Fulfillment
Poland Sp. z o.o., Wrocław